A Split In The Middle
The Making Of The Political Centre In Iran
1987-2004

Kingshuk Chatterjee

KW Publishers Pvt Ltd
New Delhi

in association with

Calcutta University
Kolkata

The Court of Directors of the East India Company sent a despatch in July, 1854 to the Governor-General of India in Council, suggesting the establishment of the Universities of Calcutta, Madras and Bombay.

In pursuance of that despatch, the University of Calcutta was founded on January 24, 1857.

The University adopted in the first instance, the pattern of the University of London and gradually introduced modifications in its constitution.

© 2012, University of Calcutta

All rights reserved. No part of this publication may be reproduced, stored in a retrieval system, or transmitted in any form or by any means, electronic, mechanical, photocopying, recording or otherwise, without the prior written permission of the copyright owner.

The views expressed in this paper are those of the author and do not represent the views of the University of Calcutta.

ISBN 978-93-81904-11-4

Contents

I. Introduction   1

II. Quis Custodiet Ipsos Custodes:
Institutional Character of the Islamic Republic   3

III. The Politics of two Extremes in the Khomeini Era   7

IV. Shifting Extremes: the Era of Rafsanjani   17

V. The Era of Hope and Despair: The Khatami Years   33

VI. Conclusion   47

A Split In The Middle
The Making Of The Political Centre In Iran: 1987-2004

I. Introduction

In 1997, Sayyid Muhammad Khatami won a landslide victory in the Presidential Elections, winning more than twenty million of the twenty-nine million votes cast. The outcome was hailed by a large number of observers as a decisive mandate for sweeping reforms in the Islamic Republic. Khatami's victory was followed by the victory of votaries of reform in the *Majlis*. The period ushered in an era of hope and heightened expectations among the post-revolutionary generation of Iranians. People began to speak of a spring after an unduly prolonged winter that had begun in 1979. Within eight years, the euphoria powering the reformist cause had disappeared; the reformists had lost the control of the *Majlis* to more conservative counterparts, and a hardliner populist Mahmoud Ahmedinejad succeeded the reformist Khatami – the spring did not last nearly as long as the winter had. The waxing and waning of the reformist movement in Iran however is probably more significant than it appears. It is not 'a dream and its death' as some Iranians like to call it; it marks instead the rise of a political centre that the Islamic Republic witnessed for the first time since the Islamic Revolution of 1979.

The political dynamics of the Islamic Republic has been considerably turbulent right from 1979. Despite the projection of a monolithic ideological façade by the regime from the autumn of 1979, the revolution itself was brought about by a range of opposition movements, not all of which was Islamic, and only one component of which was actually led by the Shi'i *'ulema* under Khomeini. Accordingly, a fierce power struggle occurred between the constitutional democrats and the *'ulema* hierocracy during the early years of the Republic, till the *'ulema* progressively consolidated their stranglehold behind the cover of the national emergency caused by the Iraqi invasion in 1980. The experience of the Iran-Iraq war served a lot to disfigure the potentials of the revolution of 1979, to the extent that one might argue that 'normal' politics resumed in Iran only after the end of the war in 1988. Because of the 'abnormality' of wartime Iranian politics, the principal political positions belonged to two ends of the political spectrum: the clergy-dominated conservative right-wing (led by the likes of President 'Ali Khamenei, now the Supreme Leader of the Republic) and the radical revolutionaries of the Islamic left-wing (led by last Prime Minister Hussein-Musavi). Despite an assortment of pragmatist individuals like Akbar Hashmi Rafsanjani, however, any trace of an organised centrist political movement was hard to detect in Iranian politics till after the death of Ayatollah Khomeini in 1989.

The literature on domestic politics of the Islamic Republic generally attributes the absence of politically centrist ideologies in two different ways. Some observers emphasise the institutional peculiarities of the Islamic Republic, which tends to facilitate rampant factionalism and polarisation of ideological positions, thereby impeding the emergence of a political middle.[1] Others tend to argue that the doctrinaire Islamist character of the revolutionary generation makes them extremely reluctant to allow any significant change in the scheme of things in the Islamic regime. The regime, therefore, promotes an equally doctrinaire opposition that chooses to spurn many of the Islamist assertions of the ruling conservatives. In this mode of analysis, a centrist political position is still some distance off in the Islamic Republic.[2]

This paper means to argue that the politics of the Islamic Republic in the post-Iraq-War era has actually witnessed the emergence of a centrist political ideology, and that despite apparent weakening of this centrist 'reformist' position towards the end of Muhammad Khatami's presidential tenure in 2005, the Iranian political centre is here to stay. The paper also means to argue that the reason why this emergence of the political centre is not immediately noticeable is primarily because the two extremes in the political arena of the Islamic Republic are not the conventional 'right' and 'left' associated with most polities. Because of historical reasons peculiar to the political trajectory of Iran in the 20th century, Iran has its social conservatives split among free-marketers and hard-line populists who make up the two extremist forces in the polity, while a large chunk of the Iranian left has become de-radicalised to the extent that at present it actually represents the middle-ground rather than an extreme position.

II. Quis custodiet ipsos custodes: Institutional character of the Islamic Republic

The institutional character of the Islamic Republic was heavily influenced by the experience of Pahlavi monarchy. The *Mashruteh* (Constitutional) Revolution of 1906 had successfully established the principle of popular sovereignty in Iranian politics.[3] Carrying the principle to its logical conclusion, in 1925, the incumbent Qajar dynasty was replaced by the house of Pahlavi by means of a plebiscite, with an agenda of developing Iran as a *modern* nation-state. Even as the Pahlavis set out to modernise Iran, they systematically undermined the institutional apparatus of legislative control over the executive. During the rule of Reza Shah, most *Majlis* (Parliament) elections were rigged almost as a matter of routine, ensuring a pliant majority that would rubber-stamp any measure solicited by the Shah.[4] It was only when the Shah was not strong enough to exert such control over the body-politic that the *Majlis* regained some temporary significance – viz. during 1941-53, the first twelve years of the reign of Muhammad Reza Pahlavi culminated in the nationalisation of Iran's oil industry under Premier Muhammad Mossadeq. Barring such exceptional stretches of weak executive authority, the Pahlavi era was characterised by virtually relentless marginalisation of the institutional checks on executive authority, and subversion of the principle of popular sovereignty. The Pahlavi regime, in fact, made use of the state apparatus to promote the interests of the ruling classes. Hence, a number of Iranians developed a deep-seated misgiving about the efficacy of the principle of separation of powers between elected legislative and executive organs of government. In 1979, therefore, after the Islamic Revolution overthrew the Pahlavis and the new regime was being shaped, a return to the *Mashruteh* notions of a simple supremacy of the legislative organ was ruled out. While the principle of elective legislative and executive authorities was retained, Ayatollah Khomeini's theory of *Vilayat-e Faqih* (Rule of the Jurist) was foisted on this institutional combine from above. The consequent amalgam of democratic and so-called 'theocratic' features has come to lend the Islamic Republic a distinctive character.

Following the principle of the *Vilayat-e Faqih*, Article 5 of the Constitution vests in a just and pious jurist (*Faqih-ye 'adl wa mutlaq*) the office of the *Rahbar* (Supreme Leader or Guide), answerable only to the God and the Imams. The *Rahbar* is the highest constitutional authority in the land despite not being democratically elected by the people.[5] He is authorised to delineate the general policies of the Islamic Republic and supervise its proper functioning. The *Rahbar* is the supreme commander of the armed forces in the Islamic Republic, and is accordingly authorised to declare war, peace and mobilisation of armed forces. He is also authorised to appoint a large number of constitutional functionaries – the commanders of armed forces, head of the judiciary, the *fuqaha* (Islamic jurists) on the Guardians Council – who are accountable only to the *Rahbar*.[6]

Chief among the democratic elements in the Islamic Republic of Iran is the popularly elected *Rais* (President).[7] Elected for a four-year term allowing only one consecutive re-election, the President appoints a council of ministers to help him discharge the functions of his office, which include determining programmes and policies of the government and implementation of laws passed by the *Majlis*. The President is responsible for the national budget, planning, law and order, defence and foreign relations of the Republic. He is also responsible for the process of recruitment, appointment and removal of public servants in all government organs.[8]

Apart from the office of the President, the *Majlis-e Showra-ye Islami* (Islamic Consultative Assembly), the supreme legislative organ in the Islamic Republic, is also directly elected by the people under a system of universal adult franchise.[9] The *Majlis* is the most important legislative organ in the Republic, within limits prescribed by the constitution. It is authorised to make laws pertaining to all matters within the compass of the state, provided the laws do not run contrary to the essence (*usul al-din*) and injunctions (*ahkam*) of the official religion, that is, Twelver Shi'ism, and are in conformity to the spirit of the constitution. In a bid to establish a democratic check on the executive, the Presidential council of ministers have to be individually approved by the *Majlis* before they assume their responsibilities. Further, at any stage, a motion of no-confidence can be brought against ministers individually or collectively, which may even lead to their removal.[10] This particular dispensation of executive and legislative powers, modelled upon the French system of the Fifth Republic, conforms to the legacy of the *Mashruteh* Revolution of 1906 with its emphasis on popular sovereignty.

However, given the experience of abuse of executive authority and subversion of the *Majlis* under the Pahlavis, the Constitution of the Islamic Republic has created an institutional complex where powers of the elected executive and legislative institutions are circumscribed by the powers and functions of a set of non-representative institutions and bodies. Among the more important of these are the *Showra-ye Negahban* (Guardians Council) and the *Majme'-ye Tashkhish-e Maslihat-e Nizam* (Expediency Council).

The *Showra-ye Negahban* (hereafter, the Guardians) is a non-representative body of twelve-members that circumscribes the authority of the *Majlis*.[11] All legislative measures passed by the *Majlis* have to be reviewed by the Guardians to ensure the compatibility of such measures with both Islam and the Constitution of the Islamic Republic, and they are further vested with the responsibility of interpretation of the Constitution.[12] Still more significantly, the Guardians are authorised to screen the candidates for the Presidency, the *Majlis*, the *Khobregan* and the various other elective offices at national and regional levels, and (arguably) to eliminate candidates with either doubtful Islamic credentials or doubtful loyalty towards the Islamic Republic.

The *Majme'-ye Tashkhish-e Maslihat-e Nizam* (lit. Council for Determination of Expediency of the System, hereafter, Expediency Council) is a body set up by an amendment to the constitution upon the instructions of the *Rahbar*, Ayatollah Khomeini, in 1988 to prevent deadlock between the *Majlis* and the Guardians. Comprising of thirty odd members (some ex officio but mostly nominated by the *Rahbar*), the Expediency Council is authorised to resolve conflicts or disputes over legislation between the

Majlis and the Guardians, and provide a binding resolution. It also functions as an advisory body for the *Rahbar*.[13]

While all these representative and non-representative bodies are directly subject to the authority of the *Rahbar*, the office of the *Rahbar* itself is supervised by the *Majlis-e Khobregan* (Assembly of Experts, hereafter Experts), a body of eighty-odd members directly elected by the people for a term of eight years. Meeting at least once in every six months, the Experts are responsible for the selection, supervision and removal of the Leader; thereby, allowing for the institutional mechanism to keep the *Rahbar* himself in check.

The institutional complex brought into being by the Islamic revolution in the body-politic of Iran was, clearly, devised with the express purpose of preventing any single institution from becoming powerful enough to dominate the rest. Even the office of the *Rahbar*, the repository of the greatest range of powers in the Islamic Republic, was used sparingly during the Khomeini years (1979-89) primarily to maintain a balance between the various political forces and government organs, rather than to be politically proactive. In absence of any single centre of authority, the Islamic Republic of Iran has evolved into a polycratic system characterised by an unrelenting struggle for power among the *Rahbar*, the President, the *Majlis* and the Guardians where each has proved perfectly willing to align with everyone else for the short term. Hence, the Rafsanjani Presidency (1989-97) was marked by close cooperation between the *Rahbar* and President but bitter opposition from the *Majlis*; the Khatami years (1997-2005) by contrast had the *Rahbar* align himself with the Guardians against the President and the *Majlis*; the Ahmedinejad era (2005 onwards) is characterised by the President being locked into combat with all the other three organs. A very telling quip about Iran's body politic says that, Iran is probably the only country in the world where a directly elected President is actually the leader of the opposition.

Yet, another expression of the revolutionary determination to prevent any possibility of concentration of power is the lack of party system in politics, lest there be domination by any one party or ideology at the expense of all others. Like-minded individuals frequently tend to gather themselves around loose political platforms or movements, such as the *Kargozaran* led by Akbar Hashmi Rafsanjani during and after his stint as the President (1989-1997). Such platforms/movements work with a reasonably clearly defined agenda – viz. the *Kargozaran* pushed an agenda of liberalisation of economy and society in a bid to rebuild the country ravaged by the war with Iraq. However, these platforms are never formally constituted into the tighter organisation that characterise political parties. As a consequence, politics in the Islamic Republic revolves around loose factions pushing particular agenda, rather than around political parties motivated by a well-defined ideology.

Partly as a result of this factional character of politics in the Islamic Republic, political observers outside the country are hard-put to characterise Iranian political formations in a manner intelligible to the outside (primarily western) world. Such attempts confuse more issues than they resolve, because even the most elementary classification of political positions into right-wing, left-wing and centre can not be appositely applied in the Iranian context. Any such attempt requires a nuanced understanding of the dynamics of politics in the Islamic Republic.

III. The politics of two extremes in the Khomeini era

The political dynamism of the Islamic Republic stems from the multiple political agenda that had driven the Islamic Revolution of 1979. The pre-revolutionary regime of the Pahlavi dynasty had set itself the task of 'modernising' Iran by implementing a linear developmental model patterned on industrialisation and social change. Powered by the ever-growing oil revenue, the Pahlavi state had become financially independent of the domestic social groups, and therefore, also less mindful of the concerns of such social groups about the character of modernisation. Such concerns included not simply economic issues (viz. the manner of sectoral allocation of oil revenue; government attempts to control the domestic market; generation of employment for growing numbers of college and university educated students), but also political issues (viz. the authoritarian disposition of the government; the degree of concentration of authority in the central government; standardisation and enforced integration of linguistic and ethnic minorities) as well as cultural (viz. westernisation and forcible secularisation of the public space). When Pahlavi modernisation programme slowed down around 1976-77 in the context of falling oil revenues, the resistance to the regime snowballed into a broad-ranging social coalition embracing the traditional business class of the *bazaaris*, the working class, students, professionals, and the urban poor, each with a different set of objectives.[14] Therefore, once the revolution took place and the new regime was founded, it was fairly certain that the concerns of all such groups would find some representation in Iranian political life. Ironically, however, in many ways the Islamic regime continues to address the issues of governance in a manner reminiscent of the previous era. Accordingly, the political agenda of the Islamic Republic exhibits a degree of continuity with the pre-revolutionary era, although there is occasionally a marked difference in the manner in which such agenda is articulated in the Islamic Republic.

The economic character of the Islamic regime quickly emerged among the central preoccupations of the revolutionaries in 1979, determined to break with the Pahlavi era. The Pahlavi state used to intervene extensively in the functioning of Iranian economy, pumping oil revenue into heavy and consumer goods industry alike, generating a prodigious degree of industrial activity and expanding economic opportunities in the country, particularly in the urban areas. The benefits of such expansion in the scope of economy, however, were reaped mostly by a small segment of technocrats, bureaucrats, industrialists and cronies of the Shah, leaving a large segment of the educated and young population of the country disgruntled with the regime. Similarly, there was little trickle-down effect for the masses of urban poor that provided the supply of labour which was crucial to the economy. Parallel to this, the regime had systematically marginalised the *bazaar* (the market area which was traditionally the hub of commercial activities in the country) by regulating the *asnaf* (guilds) and imposing price-control at times of price rise; such interventionist practices had peaked in 1976-78. The Islamic regime was expected somehow to address all of these concerns.

In response to these expectations, Islamic populism emerged as a major revolutionary agenda in the first post-revolutionary decade. Representing primarily the educated youth and the urban poor, Islamic socialists comprised of a broad-ranging group of people with a redistributive agenda, determined to redress the problems of economic inequality that characterised Pahlavi Iran. In the initial stages, they encouraged the appropriation of the resources of the various *bonyad-ha* (foundations) and redistributing that wealth among the people; they were also instrumental in the nationalisation of the assets of the 51 largest industrialists in the early months of the revolution.[15] Subsequently, after the outbreak of the Iraq-Iran war, the need to reorient economy towards the war and the crisis occasioned by the flight of managerial professionals after the revolution necessitated nationalisation of major sectors of the economy, including all private banks, insurance companies, all heavy industries (including mining and metal industries as well as plane, ship and automobile manufacturing plants).[16] This strengthened the votaries of Islamic populism who favoured the idea of a heavily regulated economy. Prominent protagonists of this agenda included Ayatollahs Mohammad Beheshti and Hossein 'Ali Montazeri, Mir Hussein-Musavi (Prime Minister 1981-89), Behzad Nabavi, *Hojjatulislam* Muhammad Muasvi-Khoeiniha, Mehdi Karrubi. All of them were associated with *Hizb-e Jomhuri-ye Islami* (Islamic Republic Party, or IRP), set up in 1979 by close followers of Khomeini to confront other political formations (Islamic, secular, and Marxist alike) from the pre-revolutionary era in order to firmly establish the principle of the *vilayat-e faqih*. They were also associated with a minority wing in the more conservative platform of *Jame'h-ye Rowhaniyat-e Mobariz*. In common parlance, this populist faction is referred to as the left-wing in post-revolutionary Iranian politics, which dominated the *Majlis* during 1981-89. Following the populist school (*maktab*) in Islamic thinking represented by Khomeini himself, these Islamic populists called themselves *Maktabi*.

The agenda of Islamic populism, though, met with considerable resistance from within the IRP itself, let alone those outside it. Representing principally the conservative interests of the *bazaar*, a very powerful faction within the IRP advocated the sanctity of private property, opposed state intervention in the economy and state taxation of the private sector. This faction of the IRP, accordingly, resented the imposition of stringent economic regulations during the war with Iraq and was instrumental in pushing through the programme of liberalisation of Iran's economy at the end of the war in 1988. Led in the initial stages by powerful ideologues of the Islamic state such as Ayatollah Morteza Motahhari, this minimalist position of the state was championed all through the 1980s by Ayatollah Muhammad Yazdi, Musavi-Ardabili, as also prominent political figures like 'Ali Khamenei (President 1981-89, *Rahbar* 1989 till date) and 'Ali Akhbar Nateq-Nouri (Speaker of the *Majlis*, 1989-97). All of them were associated with the dominant faction within the *Jame'h-ye Rowhaniyat-e Mobariz* (Society of the Combatant Clergy, hereafter JRM), an organisation which in common parlance is considered to constitute the backbone of the right-wing in Iran after 1979. The *Jamiyat-e Mo'talefeh-ye Islami* (Allied Islamic Society, hereafter the *Mo'talefeh*) – dominated by lay Islamists like Mohsen Rafiqdust (later, head of the *Bonyad-e Mustazafin*) and brothers 'Ali and Javed Larijani – was the other principal platform of the conservatives, which became more prominent during and after the Rafsanjani era.

In the first few years of the Islamic Republic, the divisions over the economic issues were downplayed by the need for the followers of Khomeini to stick together. In 1979, they successfully battled together the secularist, democratic and Marxist components of the revolutionary movement to introduce the principle of *vilayat-e faqih*. Moreover, the growing demands of regional autonomy from Iranian Azerbaijan, and demands of regional devolution of power reversing decades of centripetalism prompted both the Islamic populists and the conservatives associated with the IRP to set up a series of revolutionary institutions. The leftist-dominated revolutionary courts that dispensed rough-and-ready 'justice' by executing scores of 'collaborators' of the previous regime, the '*ulema*-dominated *komitehs* (revolutionary committees set up in localities to exercise vigil, identify enemies of the revolution and hand them over to the revolutionary courts), the *Sepah-e Pasdaran-e Inqilab-e Islami* (Islamic Revolutionary Guards Corps, or the IRGC, hereafter the *Sepah*) were all set up during the tumultuous days of 1979. When the war with Iraq began, it was used by the *Vizarat-e Ittela'at va Amniyat-e Keshvar* (Ministry of Intelligence and Security of the Realm, the VAVAK, the dreaded successor of the notorious SAVAK) as a smokescreen to eliminate all serious domestic political opposition to the '*ulema*-dominated regime using the triad of the revolutionary courts-

komiteh-Sepah: Constitutionalists like the *Nehzat-e Azadi-ye Iran* (Freedom Movement of Iran) of the Prime Minister of the interim government, Mehdi Bazargan, were repeatedly denied government offices because of 'unsuitable views', and were also persecuted; socialist revolutionaries and Islamic-Marxist guerrillas of the *Sazman-e Mojahedin-e Khalq* (Mojahedin-e Khalq Organisation or the MKO) were executed in droves, and the rest driven into exile in Iraq; the state apparatus and educational institutions, especially at the level of universities, were purged of recalcitrant liberal elements or forced to conform – all these developments were together known as the so-called *Inqilab-e Farhangi* (Cultural Revolution).[17]

By 1983, most domestic challenges to the regime were effectively neutralised. The *Sepah*, meanwhile, continued to grow, because apart from its services on the Iraq front, it also helped stave off another major crisis that was looming at the domestic front. Iranian economy was badly disrupted first by the revolution, and then by the war: in 1982, there was a 20 per cent decline in industrial production from 1977 levels, and the number of industrial wage-workers declined from over a million to a little over eight-hundred thousand.[18] A large body of the Iranian youth, mostly of the middle and lower-middle classes who would have been otherwise left unemployed, had joined the *Sepah* during the war.[19] Having particularly distinguished itself as much at home fighting internal enemies as it did fighting the Iraqis on the front, the *Sepah* secured for itself a degree of credibility in the eyes of regime and even of the people, which it subsequently converted into political capital. In course of the war, therefore, the *Sepah* began to support the Islamic socialists' agenda of state intervention in the economy, and with the support of Islamic socialists in the *Majlis* the *Sepah* even began to engage in economic activities using resources nationalised by the regime during the war. While some of the initial ventures undertaken by the *Sepah* related strictly to wartime needs of arms and ammunition, it began to branch out into legitimate chemical (allegedly as a cover for its chemical weapons factories) and mining sectors. By the time the war came to an end, the votaries of an interventionist order were quite powerful.

While the *Sepah* supported state interventionism in the 1980s, the *bonyads* (foundations) began to work against such agenda by the 1982-83.[20] Beneficiaries of billions of dollars of assets of the royal family and the exiled pre-revolutionary elites seized by the revolutionaries, the *bonyads* were dominated by powerful figures from within the clerical establishment (such as Akbar Hashmi Rafsanjani) as much as those from other social groups who became/remained close to the clerical establishment, such as the *bazaaris*. Attempts by Islamic populists in the Hussein-Musavi government, with support from the *Majlis*, to extend government control, or at the very least supervision, caused a great deal of resentment in the *bonyads*. The resentment increased when, in 1984, the highly successful *bonyad Jihad-e Sazandegi* (Reconstruction Crusde) was taken over by the government, and turned into the ministry of rural development. The more important among these *bonyads*, such as the *Bonyad-e Mostazafin wa Janbaz* (hereafter, *Mostazafin*) were determined not merely to escape government control, but even supervisory restraints such as audit.[21] Accordingly, the *bonyads* began to beef up the right-wing elements of the JRM, and auxiliary outfits such as the *Mo'talefeh*.

The divide over the economic agenda had an interesting fall-out in politics. The populist camp being led by the Prime Minister Hussein-Musavi, a large number of fairly radical legislations were proposed, despite the reluctance of the conservative President 'Ali Khamenei. Predominance of populist members in the first two *Majlis* (1981-85, 1985-89) after the revolution helped their fairly easy passage despite opposition from the conservative deputies. Unable to stall such measures in the *Majlis*, the conservatives resorted to the Guardians where all six clerical members were conservatives. Accordingly, the Guardians objected to 102 of 370 bills of the first *Majlis*, and 118 of the 316 passed by the second on the grounds of their being un-Islamic or unconstitutional.[22] In such cases of constitutional deadlock the role of Akbar Hashmi Rafsanjani (the powerful Speaker of the Parliament, 1981-89), President Khamenei and especially Khomeini himself became crucial. While Khamenei, being opposed to the principle of state regulation had little acceptability among majority of the *Majlis* deputies, Rafsanjani gained in stature as a pragmatist willing to oscillate between the conservatives and the populists, and have things resolved through mediation. Although Khomeini seldom intervened effectively except to check the growing powers of any one organ of the government, yet his inclination to favour the populist position was not lost on the Guardians.[23] Thus, once the principle of *Vilayat-e faqih* was secured, and the regime seemed to be holding its own by 1982-83, the conservatives opened the question of the nature of the *vilayat* in a bid to restrict the powers of the *Rahbar*.

In his lectures on *hokumat-e Islami* (Islamic government) during 1967-70, Khomeini had left a lot of ambiguities on what he meant by the principle of *vilayat-e faqih* – whether the supreme jurist would actually *rule*, or would he merely govern. Among Khomeini's followers, many subscribed to the position of *fiqh-e sunnati* (traditional [interpretation of] *fiqh*) – that is the *ahkam al-avvaliyeh* (primary ordinances) based on the Qur'an and the *Sunnah*) provide sufficient means to govern an Islamic society, following the original model set down by the Prophet at Medina; *ahkam-e sanaviyeh* (secondary ordinances) are permissible only in special circumstances where there is an overriding necessity for such ordinances. Other followers of Khomeini subscribed to the notion of *fiqh-e puya* (dynamic *fiqh*) – that is *ahkam-e avvaliya* provide the bedrock of Islamic legislation, not its entire structure. With changing times, Muslims in different historical conjunctures are faced with new situations; the *shari'ah* accordingly needs to adapt with changing times, producing new decrees (hence, dynamic) that comprise the *ahkam-e sanaviyeh*.[24]

By and large, the populists and left-leaning radicals in the revolutionary establishment were favourably disposed towards the idea of a dynamic *faqih*, who would generously introduce new (secondary) ordinances to facilitate state intervention in all reaches of the society in order to guarantee its 'Islamic' character. The conservatives assailed this position almost every time Khomeini's intervention was sought and secured after the *Majlis* and the Guardians faced a deadlock. They pointed out that while the 'primary ordinances' were primary (therefore essential) to the faith, 'secondary ordinances' being devised to meet particular needs were *impermanent*. These were, therefore, of political significance, and not of religious significance. This meant that what is 'necessary' in one circumstance need not be necessary at another. In other words, since dynamism of *fiqh* has no bearing on the *usul al-din* (essentials of the faith), interventions by the *Rahbar* should be sparing because he is supposed to provide religious guidance, not political leadership.

To begin with, such conservative interpretation of the nature of the *vilayat-e faqih* seemed to be endorsed by Khomeini himself. Commenting on the need for enacting land reforms in 1981, for instance, he clearly stated: "The enactment and execution of those laws on which the survival of the regime depends are permissible on a *temporary* basis and *so long as* there is an overriding need."[25] [Emphasis added]. Clearly, he was not providing religious guidance on this matter; rather, a political one. But, given the growing conflicts between the *Majlis* and the Guardians and a systemic failure in resolving these, Khomeini himself is supposed to have become concerned about the apparatus of governance. Accordingly, in the last two years of his life Khomeini became more and more openly supportive of the principle of the dynamic *fiqh*. It has even been said that Khomeini's acceptance of terms for ceasefire with Iraq 'set the tone for a less revolutionary, more temperate, and ultimately more pragmatic post-war [sic] Iran'.[26]

The changes might be said to have been set in motion when Khomeini acceded to the request from Rafsanjani and Khamenei to dissolve the IRP in May 1987, once it was clear that the rift between the populists and the conservatives made it difficult for them to operate under the party's rubric.[27] Fall in oil prices in 1986, galloping rate of inflation at 26 per cent and an even higher rate of unemployment had all indicated that the regime needed change. In December 1987, responding to a ministerial query, Khomeini took the position that the government can impose *any* regulation for the purpose of better governance. When the Guardians sought a clarification whether this meant that even the fundamental traditional laws of the faith could be replaced by state ordinances, Khomeini made probably his most categorical statement ever:

The *hokumat* [government] that is a part of the absolute vice-regency of the Prophet of God is one of the *ahkam-e awaliyeh* [primary injunctions] of Islam and has priority over all other secondary injunctions, even prayers, fasting and Hajj. The ruler is authorised to demolish a mosque or a house that is in the path of a road and to compensate the owner for his house. The ruler can close down a mosque if need be, or can even demolish a mosque that is a source of harm if its harm can not be remedied without demolition. The government is empowered to unilaterally revoke any shari'ah agreement that it has conducted with the people when those agreements are contrary to the interests of the country or of Islam.[28]

Arguing as he did, Khomeini seemed to be giving sweeping new powers to the *faqih*, that is, the office of the *Rahbar*. Simultaneously, however, he was also undermining the religiousness of the regime by arguing that the *usul al-din* (primary obligations of the faith) were secondary in comparison with the *raison d'état*.

The conservatives refused to relent. Comparing Khomeini's ruling with the food and water needed to survive in life, Ayatollah Ahmad Azari-Qomi pointed out that 'secondary ordinances are unique in that they are temporary and aim to serve immediate needs'.[29] In December 1987, Khomeini had further annoyed the conservatives defending screening of western films, saying such films could be educational, and that depiction of inadequately covered women was not a problem if they were not seen 'with lustful eyes'.[30] In August 1988, he even approved game of chess and trading in musical instruments as long as they were used for religiously sanctioned purposes. This ruling caused a considerable furore within Khomeini's own powerbase, the *howzeh* (seminary) and the conservative Qom '*ulema* were aghast. In October 1988, when Hojjatulislam Muhammad Hussein Qadiri pointed out that even the Imams considered chess as a gambling tool and music as forbidden, Khomeini said, "Based on your views, modern civilisation must be annihilated and we must all go to live forever in caves and deserts. I advise you to consider God and not be influenced by the 'pseudo-religious' and 'uneducated' *akhunds* [clergy]."[31]

If there was ever any ambiguity in his position towards the conservatives, Khomeini removed them all in February 1989, four months before his death:

> There are people in the howzeh who, while pretending to be highly

religious, are eradicating religion, the revolution and the system... Through their deceit, in universities and *howzehs* these pseudo-religious people destroy the essence of the revolution and Islam from within. With self-righteous faces and in support of religion and *Vilayat* [of the *faqih*], they accuse everyone of irreligiousness. ... I believe in *fiqh-e sunnati va javaheri* (traditional and essential jurisprudence] and agree that it is the correct and proper form of *ijtihad*. However, this does not mean that Islamic *fiqh* is not dynamic [*puya*]. Time and place are two decisive components of *ijtihad*.[32]

Such a clear-cut position persuaded the conservatives to dig their heels. Earlier, Khomeini authorised the institution of the Expediency Council to enable the government to function bypassing the Guardians if need be. Further, on the eve of elections for the third *Majlis* (1988-92), Khomeini's open support for the populist sections proved useful in their sweep of the polls. Hence, in 1989, when Khomeini ordered the establishment of *Majlis-e Baznegari-ye Qanun-e Asasi* (Assembly for the Reappraisal of the Constitution, hereafter *Baznegari*) to resolve constitutional ambiguities, the conservatives moved in for the kill. The constitution as it was revised in 1989, and as it now stands, no longer required the *Rahbar* to be a *mujtahid*; instead he is supposed to be a *faqih* (jurist) of political sagacity. The religious significance of the office of the *Rahbar* was thus dramatically reduced, pushing forth the idea of *fiqh-e sunnati*. At the same time, however, the conservative character of the clerical Assembly of Experts made it most likely that the next *Rahbar* would be conservative in his orientation; hence, political powers of the *Rahbar* were enhanced to what they are now. The assumption being, presumably, that religious authority of the *Rahbar* being not subject to any restraints except for God and the Imams, it had to be redefined within a narrower ambit; by contrast, the political decisions of the *Rahbar* could be overturned as un-Islamic if found unsuitable, hence their scope could be broadened. As a consequence the character of office of the *Rahbar* changed substantially after the Khomeini era.

The conservatives mounted an all-out offensive rallying a majority of the delegates at the *Baznegari*.[33] Anticipating the succession of 'Ali Khamenei to the office of the *Rahbar*, the conservatives pitched for the abolition of the office of the Prime Minister, and for strengthening the president as the supreme repository of executive authority.[34] This meant freeing the executive from regular scrutiny of the *Majlis*, because the Prime Minister used to be a member of, and answerable to, it. Weak parliamentary representation in the body allowed the conservatives to push the legislation through. On June 5, 1989, a day after the death of Khomeini, 'Ali Khamenei stepped down as the President of the Republic upon being chosen the new *Rahbar*. In the election that followed in July 1989, courtesy the elimination of candidature of 77 of 79 aspirants to the presidency by the Guardians, the influential speaker of the parliament Akbar Hashmi Rafsanjani won a predictable victory.

IV. Shifting extremes: the era of Rafsanjani

Rafsanjani's presidency (1989-97) was characterised by the beginning of liberalisation and the dawn of reformism in post-revolutionary Iran. It also marks the beginning of a phase when the political polarisation between the so-called right-wing and left-wing was steadily replaced by two extremes populated by the right wing with the political left scampering in the middle.

Akbar Hashmi Rafsanjani became the President of Iran at a crucial juncture in the country's history. The war with Iraq (1980-88) which cost Iran 2,13,000 lives, had damaged the country's economy nearly as much as the credibility of the Republic fighting a fruitless war. The declining standard of living and the hardships imposed by the war generated considerable disquiet. Because of shortage of foreign currency and the persisting need for wartime mobilisation, imports of items of mass consumption, which were essential for meeting domestic shortages, declined by nearly 50 per cent between 1983 and 1988.[35] Additionally, the government had to keep on raising indirect taxes and the price of state-run public utilities in order to meet its budget deficit. The acute shortage of foreign exchange (principally owing to the US sanctions on Iran since the hostage crisis of 1979) and the chronic deficiency of domestic capital mobilisation owing to the war forced the Islamic Republic to abandon one of the cardinal revolutionary principles, viz. rejection of foreign capital. All though the matter was kept secret, it was subsequently revealed that in 1989 Iran had a foreign debt of US$ 12 billion on account of its short-term borrowing.[36] The First Economic Plan (1989-93) approved by the *Majlis* projected a US$ 28 billion external borrowing for the period of the plan.[37] In order to ensure the inflow of such amount of foreign exchange, Iran sought economic consultation and policy advice form the World Bank and IMF.[38] It was clear to a large segment of the Iranian establishment that a major structural adjustment of the country's economy was a necessary precondition to approaching such international organisations. Rafsanjani, reputed for his pragmatism and ability to mediate between the conservatives and the populists, was the favoured choice of both the wings to carry this programme of liberalisation through.

Upon his ascendancy to the presidency, Rafsanjani launched the First Five Year Development Plan, known in Iran as the *asr-e sazendagi* (the era of reconstruction).[39] For nearly a decade, the government had controlled domestic prices and imposed a wage ceiling, and kept the foreign exchange rates artificially overvalued, subjected imports to government allocation, required a variety of permits for establishing new industrial enterprises, refused to allow foreign investments in Iran, and provided subsidies for nearly all basic foodstuffs. Moreover, the government transferred management of industries to the young inexperienced revolutionaries while nearly a million professionals fled the country. The policy of economic liberalisation that Rafsanjani pursued was in effect a reversal of the command economy that had been built-up incrementally in course of the 1980s. It was premised upon foreign exchange liberalisation, decontrol of prices, and elimination of subsidies and privatisation of state-owned enterprises.[40] The emphasis lay in changing the role of the state from intervention and control to supervision, thereby allowing private capital and market to increase investment in infrastructure and industrial output. Additionally, gradual reduction of dependence on oil revenue and an increase in state revenue through taxation was proposed.[41] As Mehdi Moslem puts it, this was the beginning of 'deradicalisation' of the revolution when the Islamic socialist agenda of the revolution began to be dismantled.

The conservative right pledged unanimous support for Rafsanjani's policy of economic liberalisation under the First Five Year Plan. However, echoing the misgivings of the *bazaar* which was otherwise energised by the proposed reforms, the conservatives voiced their displeasure with government plans to institute a system of progressive taxation. The left, on the other hand, bitterly disapproved of most of the reforms, issuing dire warnings that the state was caring more about economic output than socio-economic justice. The hardliner cleric Sadeq Khalkhali even warned that in the new economy, the government and the *bazaaris* planned to divide the country's resources among themselves.[42] In an interesting comment on the reforms, therefore, while being generally critical of the reforms for precisely the same reasons that the conservatives found it praiseworthy, the left-wing deputies led by Hadi Ghaffari supported progressive taxation as the only means of combating the economic domination of the rich *bazaaris*.[43]

The deradicalisation begun by Rafsanjani, however, was not confined to economics alone. Shifting his political stance markedly towards the leftist agenda of increasing the power of central executive authority, Rafsanjani attempted to address the problem of diffused public authority in the country with his efforts to circumscribe the operational freedom of revolutionary organisations. This forced him to confront the various para-governmental bodies that had come into being in course of the 1980s. One of the most significant steps in this direction was Rafsanjani's attempt in 1989 to amalgamate the military component of the *Sepah* into the professional Iranian armed forces, the *Artesh*, under the Ministry of Defence and Armed Forces Logistics. The move was only partially successful because the *Sepah* proved to be too strong to be broken up and merged with the professional *Artesh* units.[44] In 1991, regularisation of vigilante units was taken a step further when the *Niruha-ye Intezami* (Law Enforcement Forces) was created by the merger of *Komiteh* with the *gendarmerie* and the police under the rubric of the ministry of justice.[45] The leftist deputies in the *Majlis* objected to these measures because the *Sepah* and the *Komiteh* used to be dominated by Hussein-Musavi sympathisers; the conservatives did not stand in the way of these measures because of that very reason.

Other measures aiming at deradicalisation, however, proved more difficult for the conservatives to accept. The most significant in this respect proved to be the policies undertaken by the left-inclined member of JRM and Minister for Culture and Islamic Guidance, *Hojjatulislam* Sayyid Muhammad Khatami. Appointed the Minister for Culture and Islamic Guidance in 1982, Khatami was a part of the establishment that had carried out the purges of intellectual dissidents and political opponents of the Islamic Republic. From 1984, even as he defended the autocratic policies of the regime, his misgivings grew about state repression. As an *ex officio* member of the High Council of Cultural Revolution set up in that year by the order of Khomeini with Rafsanjani as its President, Khatami remarked on the need to establish an Islamic state based on pluralist ideas that he saw as the essence of Islam. By 1987, even before the end of the Iran-Iraq war, Khatami began to call for a more open cultural regime – beginning the long-winded process of something like a *glasnost* in Iran.[46] In 1988, he, along with other left-inclined members of the JRM (like Mehdi Karrubi, Muhammad Musavi-Khoeiniha, Ayatollahs Hasan Sane'i and Sadeq Khalkhali), left the outfit to set up the *Majme'-ye Rouhaniyun-e Mubariz* (Association of Combatant Clergymen, hereafter MRM).

Rafsanjani's liberalisation agenda gave Khatami the opportunity to carry out his policy of emancipation of Iran's public space: cable and satellite television was permitted in Iran for the first time during Khatami's tenure, exposing Iranians to western cultural influences; censorship was relaxed on both print and electronic media; the number of newspapers and journals published increased from 102 in 1988 to 369 in 1992.[47] In 1990, he even established a 'press jury' to investigate issues involving the media. His policies were reinforced by the stint of Rafsanjani's brother, Muhammad Hashemi, as the head of Iranian Radio and TV (*Sada wa Sima*). The conservatives opposed Khatami's programme for the liberalisation of the cultural regime but could not dislodge him from the HCCR because of the support he enjoyed from Khomeini. After Khomeini's death, Rafsanjani continued to back Khatami till the pressure became intense, and Khatami had to resign in 1992. In his last months, as the Minister for Culture and Islamic Guidance, Khatami came under sustained attack from his clerical opponents by refusing to censor foreign music video and films beamed through satellite television channels. Clerical *Majlis* deputies argued that such films and videos are 'agents of corruption and fornication.' Khatami tried in vain to explain, "If there is a dispute against a piece of film or music, we cannot declare films or music as inadmissible and thereby spoil the issue."[48] Warning that restrictive and exclusionary attitudes with different ideas to that of the regime would ultimately lead to a dictatorship, Khatami maintained that 'reedom of thought and respect for intellectual honour are among the primary goals of the revolution'.[49]

Khatami's attempt at liberalisation of the cultural policies of the Islamic Republic was opposed by two political positions. The conservatives in the *Majlis* and the Guardians – clerics of the JRM as much as the lay members of the *Mo'talefeh* – considered such policies to be *taquti* ('Satanic', a term associated with secularisation under the Shah), and condemned the laxity encouraged by the government. Significantly, the second source opposition to the cultural policies came from the socially-conservative element among the populists of the 1980s – the *Sepah*, or more exactly the *Basijis*. During the 1980s, the *Basij* forces had worked in tandem with the regime to physically crush all domestic opposition. Frequently, such activities took the form of enforcing Islamic virtues and punishing immoral or lax behaviour on part of the people, and were constitutionally underwritten by the injunction to engage in *amr beh al-ma'ruf wa nahy an'l munkar* (lit. Enjoin what is known [to be Good] and Forbidding the Evil). Determined to create a more open and free society, Rafsanjani was particularly wary of *Basij* tactics of physical assault and summary punishment. His support for the policies of Khatami, thus, was directly in opposition to modus operandi of the *Basij*.

During 1990-92, the conservative right grew determined in its opposition to Rafsanjani administration, partly because of the liberal cultural policies of Khatami, and partly because of the manner in which Rafsanjani was using the elective office of the presidency to push industrial policies that the conservatives disagreed with. The conservative response was to attempt at the consolidation of other constitutional institutions, such as the Experts and the *Majlis* using the one institution they dominated ever since 1979, the Guardians.

In July 1990, the conservative-majority of the Experts decided to change two of the laws for the election to the body that allowed the Guardians a decisive influence in the selection of candidates for the body.[50] As the left had almost no representation in the Guardians, this effectively guaranteed that the left could be excluded from the Experts as well. The left sought in vain Khamenei's intercession on their behalf; he endorsed the conservative position that the Experts being an autonomous body, they could make their own laws. In the end, the conservatives succeeded in eliminating key figures of the left from the Experts: of the 178 applicants for the 76 seats in the assembly, 62 failed the examination; prominent left-inclined clerics like Mehdi Karrubi, Musavi-Khoeiniha and Khatami did not even run for a seat in the assembly; hard-line leftists like Sadiq Khalkhali and the *Rahbar*'s own brother, Hadi Khamenei, were designated unfit to run.[51]

In December 1991, the Guardians clarified the reference to its 'supervisory' role in the *Majlis* elections of article 99 of the constitution. The Guardians announced its role to be *nezarat-e istesavi* (supervisory approval), which implied that all candidates to the *Majlis* had to be accepted by the Guardians, regardless of approval from the ministry of interior. The left tried to resist this measure by pointing out, as Musavi-Khoeiniha did, "[t]he regime belongs to the people and they are its own guardians."[52] But Khamenei's support for the conservatives proved decisive when he issued them virtually a blank cheque saying:

> If someone speaks and writes in opposition to the views of the *faqih*, he is opposed to the principle of *vilayat-e faqih*. ... As a rule, ..., it is better if you do not select these people. If there is no proof or evidence against them [being opposed to the *vilayat-e faqih*}, you can act based on your knowledge.[53]

This implied that the Guardians could use any statement critical of the institution or even the person of the *Rahbar* (that is, Khomeini or Khamenei) to disqualify a candidate from running for *Majlis*. More significantly, even if such evidence was not readily available, any insinuation of opposition to the 'Islamic' nature of the regime would suffice.

Accordingly, in the run-up to the 1992 elections, 1,060 of 3,150 registered candidates including 30 incumbent deputies were pronounced unfit to run for the *Majlis* – including leftwing heavyweights like Asadollah Bayat, Atefeh Rajaee (wife of Hussein Musavi) and Sadiq Khalkhali. Rafsanjani acceded to this veritable purge of the left from the *Majlis*, hoping it would end the resistance to his programme of economic liberalisation.[54] Many of the leftist deputies who were allowed to contest the polls eventually lost their seats, including Karrubi and Hadi Khamenei. The conservative coalition of the clergy-dominated JRM, and its predominantly lay Islamist ally the *Mo'talefeh* and other smaller outfits came to dominate the *Majlis*. For the first time since 1979, the left had lost their control over the legislative.

Right after gaining control of the *Majlis*, the conservatives mounted an attack on the liberal cultural policies of the regime. Within three months, making use of the right of interpellation (Article 89 of the constitution), the conservative majority in the *Majlis* expressed its lack of confidence in the Minister for Culture and Islamic Guidance, Muhammad Khatami. In July 1992, accordingly, Khatami had to resign, and was replaced by the prominent *Mo'talefeh* member (and son-in-law of Morteza Motahhari, one of the most prominent disciples of Khomeini) 'Ali Larijani.[55] Larijani went on to systematically dismantle Khatami's liberal cultural policies and involved conservative individuals and institutional strongholds with the making of socio-cultural policies. In December 1992, Larijani made public his ministry's intention to bankroll the mosques into becoming primary cultural headquarters.[56] In April 1993, mosque trusteeships were authorised to issue permits for printing and publishing houses and video clubs.[57] In September 1993, forty cultural centres were promised in various Tehran mosques to counter cultural blitz of the west.[58]

In his avowed agenda of curtailing *azad-andeshi* (free-thinking) Larijani enjoyed full-support of the conservatives in the *Majlis* and outside. However, given that the ministry of interior was still beyond the pale of the conservatives, enforcement of such restrictive policies became somewhat difficult. Accordingly, the traditional conservative forces decided to use the social hardliners, the *Basijis*, as their physical arm. In November 1992, the *Majlis* passed a law for the 'legal protection of the *Basijis*' authorising them to assist the law enforcement forces in fighting crimes in the country.'⁵⁹ The law, allowing the *Basijis* to become pro-active, emboldened them to manhandle individual offenders of 'Islamic sensibilities' in the name of custodianship of the Islamic character of the revolution.

The law of 1992, formalising the role of the *Basij* as an officially sanctioned vigilante organisation served a further purpose. The *Basij* had begun to lose its relevance after the end of the Iraq war, and found it reasonably difficult to reinvent itself. Unlike the main core of the *Sepah*, which had gained access to industrial and other economic enterprises, the *Basij* did not quite benefit materially from the period of economic reconstruction that characterised the Rafsanjani era. Thus, the predominantly lower-middle class elements of the *Basij* found in the November 1992 laws a vindication of its continued existence. They became crucial to the mounting conservative opposition that characterised Rafsanjani's second term. Significantly, though, by the time the Rafsanjani era came to a close, they had already established themselves as distinct from the traditional conservative forces of the JRM-*Mo'talefeh-bazaar* axis, and constituted a socially conservative but economically populist extreme in Iranian politics.

The ascendancy of the conservatives signalled by the 1992 *Majlis* elections eventually pushed Rafsanjani to the middle ground in Iranian politics, if he was not already there. His shift to the centre was largely influenced by his confrontation with the *bazaar* and its conservative allies over economic policies.

The aims of the First Five Year Plan (1989-94) had been proclaimed to be regeneration of the economy, reconstruction of the war-damaged regions, promotion of private investment, *inter alia*. The economic policies of the government seemed to be working pretty effectively till as late as 1991-92. After a slow start in 1989-90, the actual GDP growth had initially proved higher than the planned growth (11.5 per cent as against projected growth of 9.2 per cent in 1990-91 and 10.1 per cent as against 6.8 per cent projected for 1991-92). This growth, however, was powered by favourable price of oil in the global market, which helped the actual growth in the oil sector to be double the projected rate (19.9 per cent as against 9.6 per cent in 1990-91 and 11.1 per cent as against 3.4 per cent in 1991-92). The benefits of growth in oil revenues helped investment in Iranian industry which grew by 13.4 per cent (as against planned 15.2 per cent) in 1990-91 and by 17.2 per cent (as against 14.6 per cent) in 1991-92. But when the growth in the oil sector slowed down in 1992-93 (2.1 per cent as against planned growth of 11.3 per cent), industrial growth rate also fell dramatically (4.7 per cent as against 16.4 per cent).[60] While sectoral growth of economic output was thus closely linked with oil revenue earned by the state, liberalisation of the economy with its liberal import regime resulted in a different problem. At a time when Iran's total oil and non-oil exports increased from US$ 10.71 billion (1989-90) to US$ 18.66 billion (1991-92), imports increased from US$ 10.61 billion to US$ 25.2 billion over the same time frame.[61]

A major component of this import was 'excessively high private consumption' of 'final consumer goods'.[62] The beneficiaries of this sort of commercial activity being the *bazaar*, Rafsanjani's economic policies generally enjoyed conservative support till about 1991. However, a set of negative economic indicators, not the least of which was a rapid growth of the rate of inflation (50 per cent in 1992), necessitated a policy revision on part of the government. The principal problem was identified in the fact that the *bazaari*s, who made up the largest component of the private sector, made huge profits in commerce exploiting the liberal import regimes, but chose not to reinvest in domestic industrial projects. Thus of the three hundred companies and production units whose stocks were made available on the Tehran stock exchange, the shares of only 14 were brought by the private sector.[63] Given this problem of inadequate private capital investment, by mid-1991 the government resolved to exercise more control over the direction of the economy, increase revenues from public services, imposed import restrictions and increased tariffs and quotas.[64] These measures began to undermine the *bazaar* economic system.

Matters came to a head over the 1993-94 budget session of the *Majlis*. The government proposed to challenge the autonomy of the *bazaar* economic system by transferring its control on the country's capital to the government and the banks. The budget further proposed to increase revenue by 50 per cent through taxes, boost exports and – most significantly – authorising the banks to issue government bonds and allow competitive rates of interest to the public to mobilise domestic savings. While all of these were measures directly critical of the economic order favoured by the *bazaar* – an economy dominated by commercial exchange rather than industrial production – perhaps the most damaging measure for the *bazaar* was devolution and fixed-rate currency policy. With the value of the Iranian currency, the *rial*, being allowed to drop from 70 to the dollar to 1,450 to the dollar, the government emphasised its declared policy of discouraging further imports and investment in domestic industrial projects. That the budget was at all passed in spite of the fierce resistance from the *bazaaris* and their political allies in the *Majlis* was because of a clever move by Rafsanjani. He announced that government subsidies of essential goods for the following year would be doubled.[65] No matter how strident the parliamentary opposition to the budget might have been, vetoing such a bounty for the people at a time of run-away inflation would be tantamount signing a political death warrant. But the writing was clearly on the wall for Rafsanjani. The virulence of the conservative opposition to the President clearly indicated the end of their extended honeymoon.

In the 1993 presidential elections, Rafsanjani won his second term comfortably with 10 million votes (63 per cent of all votes cast). Two things were noteworthy about this election: first, despite formal support by the conservative lobby for Rafsanjani, both of the other two contenders (Ahmad Tavakkoli and Abdullah Jasbi, winning four and one million votes respectively) were conservative, and second, only 55 per cent of the total electorate actually bothered to turn up on the polling day, indicating ennui with politics in the Islamic Republic.[66] The conservatives used this to hem in Rafsanjani from the very beginning. When the President presented his council of ministers before the *Majlis*, he was given clearly to understand that ministers had to be of conservative persuasion, and the architect of his economic policy Mohsen Nurbakhsh had to go. Rafsanjani relented by reshuffling his cabinet and packing it heavily with people acceptable to the conservative-dominated *Majlis*.[67]

Despite dropping Nurbakhsh, however, Rafsanjani's determination to push forward with economic reforms ensured continued confrontation with the conservatives. The budget of 1994-95 proposed to raise fuel and energy prices substantially to finance various government projects, to control liquidity through selective credits offered by banks and tighter fiscal controls, and to decrease subsidies gradually aiming at their eventual elimination.[68] The conservative delegates of the JRM and the *Mo'talefeh* fractured these plans by resisting raising of taxes on public utilities (except utilities), imposing tax burdens on state enterprises, blaming the banks and the government's monetary policy for rampant inflation and finally forcing a 10 per cent reduction in projected state expenditure.[69]

The debates over Second Five Year Plan removed all pretence of conservative support for Rafsanjani. The *Majlis* decided to revoke all exemptions from customs, tariffs and taxes of ministries, government companies and state-run enterprises. It also sought to oblige the government bodies to obtain all their products from domestic suppliers instead of foreign outfits. Most significantly, the *Majlis* sought to slow down the industrial development that was central to the 'reconstruction' of Iran, reducing budget for various development projects by 50 trillion, diverting the money towards agriculture on the plea of helping backward areas out of their backwardness. Moreover, instead of phasing out government subsidies (thereby reducing state expenditure on economically unsustainable propositions), the *Majlis* actually proposed increasing subsidies by a third. According to a prominent conservative Asghar-Owladi, "The structural adjustment policies must be continued, but we thought they should move at slower pace."[70]

Rafsanjani retaliated with a war of attrition against the *bazaar*, the principal support base of the conservatives. In May 1994, he set up *Komiteh-ye Tanzim-e Bazaar* (Committee for Adjustment of Bazaar), aiming at controlling price fluctuations in the market and to eliminate brokers and middlemen involved in distribution and sale of merchandise. The Committee immediately instructed all producers, guilds and importers to place price tags on their products; it also instructed the government to determine the prices of 18 essential goods. Despite the outrage voiced by the *bazaar*, and the *Mo'talefeh* deputies in the *Majlis*, the ministry of commerce was authorised to arrest and punish hoarders in September 1994.[71] In December 1994, came probably the deadliest assault on the *bazaar*.

A special committee comprising of members from ministries of economics and finance, oil, industry and agriculture was formed. The committee was to supervise provision and distribution of essential goods for public factories, control overpricing and determine fair prices of goods; it was further to organise and regulate distribution channels, providing sufficient funds for creating government-run chain stores for direct supply of goods.[72] In October 1995, the *Bank Markazi* (Central Bank) forbade all purchase and sale of foreign currency outside the banking system or authorised money-changers, terminating a major component of *bazaar* activity that went back over several centuries. For Rafsanjani as much as the conservatives there could be no going back from this point on.

The final split between Rafsanjani and the conservatives, and Rafsanjani's eventual alliance with the more moderate elements of the revolutionary left-wing took place in the backdrop of a struggle for the public space in Iran as an extension of the general agenda of reconstruction under Rafsanjani.

Khatami's liberalisation of the public space in Iran had thrown up a large array of possibilities that fitted in with Rafsanjani's general take on rebuilding Iran. One of these was the beginning of something like a municipal revolution in the country. It began essentially with the appointment of the middle-aged *maktabi* Gholam-Hussein Karbaschi as the Mayor of Tehran in the winter of 1989-90, after a successful stint as the Prefect of Isfahan. Karbaschi's tenure was characterised by a rapid development of the urban infrastructure of the capital, as also creation of open public parks. The highly energetic municipal administration of Tehran under Karbaschi set an example for other municipal administrations to follow. Most major residential localities in cities in like Tabriz, Mashhad, Shiraz, etc. inevitably made similar open public spaces accessible to the people. Maintained principally by means of municipal taxes collected from citizens (*hamshahri*), these parks swiftly became a space that the citizens claimed for their own. While conservatives resented the principle of taxation that characterised this municipal revolution, inhabitants of the cities proved reasonably content with these 'pockets of freedom', exempted from being under the scrutiny of the state.[73]

The Iranian youth, in particular, found these 'pockets of freedom' exhilarating after the enforced moral strictures during the war with Iraq.

Exposed to images of the lifestyle of developed societies that was beamed into Iran through cable and satellite television during the relaxed years under Khatami, the youth in Iran availed of the various municipal parks as the arena of public sociability where the sexes could mingle at ease.[74]

In 1992, after the replacement of Khatami by Larijani, the parks began to come under fire from the conservatives as 'promoting the western culture of unfetteredness'.[75] In fact, one of the aims of the *Majlis* behind empowering the *Basij* in 1992 was to enforce restrictive Islamic morality in public spaces, such as the parks. By 1993, the alignment between the conservatives of the JRM and *Mo'talefeh* with the social hardliner *Basijis* became particularly vicious in 'turning back the cultural clock of Iran.'[76] In this moral crusade of the conservatives and hardliners, Khamenei supported the conservative cause. In June 1993, Khamenei set up a new vigilante body, the *Setad-e Yahya-ye Amr beh Ma'aruf wa Nahy az Munkar* (Headquarter for the Revival of Enjoining the Good and Forbidding Evil, hereafter *Setad*) under the staunch conservative Ayatollah Jannati.[77]

Composed primarily of recruits from the young *Basijis*, the *Setad* was sought to be used by the conservatives to undermine the cultural freedom that Khatami sought to promote. Thus the *Setad* became particularly active in the two arena where that ambience of cultural freedom had become most conspicuous – the municipal parks and the universities – and which provided the real catchments of leftist politics. With its vigilante activities given constitutional authorisation and endorsed by the conservative forces and the *Rahbar* himself, the *Basijis* in general and the *Setad* became active in endorsing a strict morality code in public place, especially in the municipal parks and the universities. The *Basijis* targeting of the universities being aimed specifically at breaking up leftist student unions under the cover of enforcement of Islamic morality (viz. segregation of the sexes in public place, proper dress code, etc), the influential student organisation *Daftar-e Tahkim-e Vahdat* (Office of Strengthening of Unity) fought out a vicious turf war in the universities. In defence of *basiji* vigilantism, the head of the *Setad*, Ayatollah Jannati pronounced at length upon the need for student associations to be under the supervision of the clergy to retain their Islamic character.[78] Khamenei himself expressed his disapproval of the weakening of the Islamic spirit in universities and emphasised the need to replace the 'ambivalent' approach of the intellectuals with the revolutionary spirit of the *Basij*.[79] Larijani used the platform of the Ministry of Culture and Islamic Guidance to spread the idea that proper culture in Iran was that of the *Basij*. In October 1993, Larijani announced that the ministry would coordinate its activities with the *Basij*.[80]

The deadliest salvo of the conservatives in this battle for the public space came in September 1993, when a report was released by a group of *Majlis* deputies detailing un-Islamic content of national TV and radio. The *Majlis* responded to this report by passing a bill to inspect the revolutionary credentials of its personnel, conformity of TV and radio programmes with the *Shari'ah*, and to ascertain if radio and TV were spreading western culture among the youth.[81] The committee found programmes to be neither revolutionary nor Islamically oriented; films screened were found to be mostly foreign ones that were un-Islamic; the personnel were found to be inadequately revolutionary in their orientation and that too many women were employed by these organisations. Worst of all, both the organisations were found guilty of improper use of funds.[82] The *Majlis* then moved a vote of no-confidence against its intended target Muhammad Hashemi, the head of Iranian TV and Radio. Soon after this, Hashemi resigned and was replaced at Khamenei's instructions by Larijani.

Larijani's successor at the Ministry of Culture and Islamic Guidance was another rigidly puritan *Mo'talefeh* member, Mustafa Mir-Salim. The new minister immediately pronounced his unqualified support for *Basiji* vigilantism, and launched a campaign of cleansing the press. In September 1994, the ministry proclaimed that only houses with religious-nationalist qualifications would be given permission to publish. Left-leaning newspapers like *Havades, Gardun, Bahman, Payam-e Daneshju* and *Aineh-ye Andisheh* were closed in close succession. The ministry also withdrew support for renowned liberal film-makers like Mohsen Makhmalbaf, Majid Majidi, and others.[83]

It was in this backdrop of simultaneous right-wing assault on the pragmatic line followed by Rafsanjani and the positions adopted by the Iranian left that Rafsanjani and the leftists came close to each other around the time of *Majlis* elections of 1996. The distance between Rafsanjani and the left had begun to narrow ever since 1993, when the President's economic policy began to emphasise the need for heavier taxation of the private sector for better societal distribution of wealth, and greater role for the state organisations in the arena of economics. The *Refah* initiative proved of particular significance as the Tehran municipality under the one-time *maktabi* Karbaschi began to work hand-in-glove with other state corporations to break the monopoly of the *bazaar*. The leftist forces too, under people like Khatami, moderated their previous opposition to economic liberalisation and foreign capital. Rafsanjani and the left had always agreed on the need for developing Iran into a powerful industrial economy. By 1993-94, the left came around to Rafsanjani's vision of mixed-economy integrated with the international economic order. Prominent figures of the left like Hussein-Musavi, Khatami and Mehdi Karrubi began to pronounce favourably about the Rafsanjani's attempts at establishing connections with international organisations like the World Bank, IMF and the WTO.[84] They even voiced their support for Rafsanjani's attempts at normalising relations with the US, reversing their hitherto strident opposition to the *shaitan-e buzurg*. A prominent left-wing journal, *Jahan-e Islam* went to the extent of arguing: "Iran cannot live in a vacuum and be oblivious to the realities of the world."[85]

The first definitive indication of a political centre in the Islamic Republic came with the foundation of the *Hizb-e Kargozaran-e Sazendegi* (Party of the Executives of Reconstruction, hereafter *Kargozaran*). On January 20, 1996, fifteen incumbent and former members of Rafsanjani's cabinet announced their decision to run for the 1996 *Majlis* elections.[86] They stated their goal to be 'to continue the post-war accomplishments of Rafsanjani's reconstruction efforts aimed at the political and economic development of Iran. ... [and to create] social justice, development without the rule of capital ... use of experts and reliance on expertise, and creation of an environment where ideas can flourish'.[87]

The *Kargozaran* decision to run for the *Majlis* was motivated principally by the desire to break the conservative stranglehold on the legislative organ, which was stonewalling Rafsanjani's reconstruction agenda. In order to reach out to the people directly, the *Kargozaran* decided to highlight the economic and social reforms achieved or advocated by Rafsanjani, and made a powerful case for a liberal democratic order resting on free civil society and mixed economy. As *Hamshahri*, the mouthpiece of Tehran municipality put it, the aim of the *Kargozaran* was 'to strengthen the *Majlis* and create a more pluralistic environment in the country.'[88] By and large, the left welcomed the entry of the *Kargozaran*. Even though some protagonists of the left continued to be critical of Rafsanjani's economic policies as too liberal, powerful figures of the MRM like the former speaker of the *Majlis*, Mehdi Karrubi, Musavi-Lari, Abdullah Nuri and Ilias Hazrati came out in favour of the *Kargozaran*. The conservatives, by contrast, were determined not to relinquish the leverage they had gained in the *Majlis*. Asghar-Owladi, a prominent *Mo'talefeh* member, for instance, attacked the *Kargozaran* decision to run as a potential violation of the principle of separation of powers between the executive and legislative organs.[89] Other *Mo'talefeh* figures repeatedly harped on the doubtful character of the allegiance of the *Kargozaran* to the principle of *Vilayat-e Faqih*; yet others identified the economic adversities of the Rafsanjani era with the body because it included people like Nurbakhsh and Muhammad Hashemi.

Conservative determination to hold on to the *Majlis* became clear when of the 5,359 candidates registered only 3,228 were approved by the Guardians. Even then, the three main forces, the JRM-*Mo'talefeh*, the MRM and its allies and the *Kargozaran* supposedly got similar share of votes and the *Majlis* looked poised to be deadlocked till the Guardians disqualified election results of 16 districts to allow the conservatives to retain their hold over the *Majlis* with the speakership going to 'Ali Akbar Nateq-Nouri. Significantly, however, in response to the JRM-*Mo'talefeh* axis that came into being in the *Majlis* as the *jame'eh-ye* Hizbullah (Society of Hizbullah), the *Kargozaran* and the Islamic left joined their forces to form the first centrist political combination – the *Majme'-ye* Hizbullah (Assembly of Hizbullah) – in the Islamic Republic on the floor of the *Majlis*.[90]

Coming to the close of the Rafsanjani years, the centrist political formation made little impression on Iranian politics right away. The centrists of the *Kargozaran*, the MRM and the student organisation of *Tahkim* began to focus instead on the next major drama on the political stage of the

Islamic Republic, the presidential election of 1997. With Rafsanjani being constitutionally debarred from a third consecutive term, both conservatives and centrists alike identified the election as crucial for their own agenda. For the centrists, the agenda was to proceed with the reform of the system launched by Rafsanjani; for the conservatives this was the best opportunity to roll it back.

Kept out of almost all locations of power in the Iranian establishment, the *Kargozaran*-left axis was determined to project an electable candidate. Its initial choice, the former Prime Minister Hussein-Musavi had some problems in this respect. Being a hardcore Islamic populist, while he was certain to get the left-leaning votes, he was not fully convincing for many as the man most likely to carry forward Rafsanjani's reforms. Moreover, Rafsanjani himself was not very enthusiastic about Hussein-Musavi's candidacy. Slated to retain the chairmanship of Expediency Council, Rafsanjani was hoping that a weak presidency deadlocked with the *Majlis* would allow him to remain relevant in Iranian politics – Musvi was unlikely to fit that part. But the nomination of Hussein-Musvi prompted the *Mo'talefeh*-JRM axis to project the powerful speaker of the *Majlis*, 'Ali Akbar Nateq-Nouri, and even the *Kargozaran*-left axis considered conservative victory almost certain. Once the *Rahbar* was heard to have said within his confidential circle that he would not allow a lay president, Hussein-Musvi decided to pull out.[91] At this stage, the grapevine began then to tout Khatami as a possible candidate of the left.[92] In January 1997, after a discussion with the *Rahbar*, Sayyid Muhammad Khatami declared himself as a candidate.[93] The *Tahkim, the* Assembly of Hizbullah and the MRM promptly declared their support for Khatami's candidacy.[94] On April 13, 1997 the Kargozaran too declared Khatami to be their candidate for the forthcoming elections.[95] The centrist political combination forged the previous year appeared to be holding. On May 23, 1997, the voters endorsed the decision by electing Khatami with the biggest ever margin for Presidential elections in the Islamic Republic.

V. The era of hope and despair: the Khatami years

Almost no one, not even *Hojjatulislam* Sayyid Muhammad Khatami himself, seems to have thought that Nateq-Nouri, having the support of the *Rahbar*

'Ali Khamenei, could be defeated.'[96] Thus, when Khatami agreed to run for the presidency, he had made it very clear to his campaign team that he was entering the arena primarily to openly discuss and raise awareness about the various structural reforms that he believed were necessary for the Islamic Republic to survive. The agenda for reforms that he drew up were anticipated and largely attempted by Rafsanjani himself, hence the *Kargozaran* came around to not only supporting Khatami but actually raise the profile of his candidature to an extent that the face of the smiling '*Mard az Yazd*' (the Man from Yazd) became a household phenomenon in Iran. Khatami, however, went beyond the limits imposed by Rafsanjani's pragmatism and spoke about a systemic reform that proposed to substantively alter the Islamic regime. Here, presumably lay the secret of Khatami's electoral landslide.

Khatami's campaign was premised upon the need for *tahamol* (toleration) as a *sine qua non* for strengthening civil society (*jame'h-ye madani*) and rule of law (*hokumat-e qanuni*) in the Islamic Republic. Careful enough not to challenge the foundational principle of the Islamic Republic, the *Vilayat-e Faqih*, Khatami claimed his agenda of institutionalisation of rule of law in Iran, and creation of a democratic order was the inherent purpose behind Ruhollah Khomeini's doctrine of rule by the Jurist. Arguing that the systematic decline in voter turn-out undermined the very legitimacy of the Islamic regime, Khatami subtly challenged the pre-dominant conservative position that the Islamic Republic derived its legitimacy primarily from Islam and not the people. Khatami argued that the Islamic Revolution of 1979 was motivated by the need to establish a democratic society, which was the defining feature of the Islamic order that Imam Khomeini had meant to institute.[97] Khatami believed the vicious political culture that had emerged in the Islamic regime, confusing dissent with enmity, undermined the very basis of that intention. He championed instead the notion of *chandarzeshi* (pluralism), which implied equal legitimacy of all the different approaches to the Islamic order, and identified the need for *tahamol* to accommodate such divergent approaches. With that aim in mind Khatami spoke of the need to strengthen the representative institutions of the presidency and the *Majlis*, and reduce the diffusion of sovereign authority by limiting the right to exercise it in the representative institutions. At the same time, instead of concentrating all powers in the hands of the President as Rafsanjani tried to, Khatami spoke of devolving power to the various levels of local government that dated back to the pre-revolutionary era. This was, clearly, in complete opposition to the closed political system that the conservatives had been developing since the death of Khomeini, based upon the notion of *jame'h-ye vilayi* (a society that needs guidance from above). By speaking of giving power back to the society, Khatami meant to assail the legitimacy sought by the conservative establishment for their domination of the institutional complex of the Islamic Republic in the name of Islam. Because of the very nature of his agenda, Khatami emerged as the personification of all the various demands for reform that were circulating in Iran – hence the 'reformist' tag attached to the political movement *Nehzat-e Dovvom-e Khordad* (Second of Khordad Movement, after the date in Persian calendar on which the Presidential election of 1997 took place) that brought Khatami to power.

Khatami's tally of over 20.7 million votes (out of a total electorate of 29.7 million) in the presidential election signified not only the largest ever reversal for the conservative establishment, but also the largest ever turnout in post-revolutionary Iranian elections. Although no rigorous psephological study has yet been made of the victory, components of the *Dovvom-e Khordad* movement can be read backwards from the subsequent shape that the verdict assumed. Votaries of economic liberalisation and industrial development that made up the *Kargozaran* constituency presumably voted for Khatami, as did the core moderate Islamic populist constituency – which together made up the political centre. In addition, a large section of the urban Iranian youth and the intelligentsia, fretful of the restrictions imposed in the name of Islamic character of the regime, and supportive of Khatami's call for *tahamol* voted for him. Also, minority communities of Iran – religious (Zoroastrians, Jews, Christians), linguistic (Turkics and Arabs) and ethnic (Kurdish) – voted in large numbers for the man they fondly remembered for reducing many of their inconveniences as the Minister for Culture and Islamic Guidance.[98] Even more significantly, an overwhelming majority of Iranian women found in Khatami's reform programme a credible means of improving the condition of women in the country. The most surprising among Khatami voters in 1997, however, were the smaller merchants of the *bazaar*, resentful as much of the regulation under Rafsanjani as of the unbridled capitalism of the bigger *bazaaris*, championed by the conservative establishment. These smaller *bazaaris* favoured Khatami's agenda of structural reform and deregulation of the Iranian economy.[99] Yet, another surprise was a split in the vote of the *Sepah* and the *Basij*, with the more populist elements favouring Khatami's agenda of social justice as a guarantee of his opposition to the unbridled capitalism favoured by conservatives like Nateq-Nouri.[100]

The broad-based social coalition that propelled the *Dovvom-e Khordad* movement represented the desire of a large segment of the Iranian society for the Islamic regime to change dramatically. In a way, the mandate that brought Khatami to power was more expansive than even that Rafsanjani enjoyed at the height of his popularity during the first term. Khatami immediately began efforts to address the expectations of the people, and became mired in a confrontation with the conservatives that ultimately exhausted the dynamism of the reformist movement, and left the centrist social coalition divided.

The *Dovvom-e Khordad* movement had stunned the conservative establishment. They had chosen Nateq-Nouri, a middle ranking cleric (*Hojjatulislam*) to confront a highly divisive lay politician Hussein-Musavi in the presidential polls. To their surprise, Nateq-Nouri ended up not only pitted against another middle-ranking cleric but one who was actually a Sayyid – something that a pious Iranian is supposed to value greatly. The landslide victory won by Khatami surprised them even further, to the extent that the conservatives actually claimed Khatami's victory as a reinforcement of the legitimacy of the Islamic order.[101] Thus, when Khatami presented his centre-left council of ministers before the conservative dominated *Majlis*, despite some debates over a couple of the appointments, all received fairly easy approval. Within months, however, the conservatives were back on a confrontational mode.

Khatami began with his agenda of strengthening the representative institutions of the Islamic Republic right away. In his first press conference five days after his election, he noted, "Our main goal is to institutionalise the rule of law and implement the constitution."[102] He went a step ahead in his inaugural address to the *Majlis*, when, paying homage to 'Ali Khamenei, he implied that the role of the *Rahbar* should be limited to supervisory-guidance, because he was the 'symbol' of national sovereignty and unity, drawing his power and legitimacy from the society as a whole and the constitution – that is, he should not take sides.[103] In November 1997, this position was considerably strengthened by an unexpected intervention from within the clergy. Ayatollah Montazeri, who at one point of time was Khomeini's designated successor to the post of *Rahbar*, blasted Khamenei and the conservatives for creating an un-Islamic authoritarian system. Questioning Khamenei's religious qualifications for the office, Montazeri warned the *Rahbar* not to meddle with the elected office of the President.[104]

The agenda received widespread support from a plethora of publications, newspapers and journals alike, for which licence was issued generously by Khatami's leftist minister for Culture and Islamic Guidance, Ataollah Mohajerani. New newspapers *Jame'h, Tus, Neshat, Khordad* and *Sobh-e Imroz*, and journals like *Rah-e Nau* and *Aban* together with established left-centrist publications like *Salaam, Iran-e Farda, Asr-e Ma* and *Kiyan*, provoked the conservatives by advocating for a supervisory *Rahbar* and a strong civil society. This was made easier by Khatami's proclamation that 'guidance' in the ministry of culture should not degenerate into guiding thinkers what to think.[105] Mohajerani followed in the footsteps of his President to proclaim his aim of turning 'the ministry of guidance into the ministry of culture.' Indeed, he launched some of the most tolerant and progressive cultural policies enacted since 1979, to the point of doing away with pre-publication censorship.[106]

In his bid to strengthen the representative organs of the Islamic Republic, Khatami championed the cause of subjecting every functionary of the Islamic regime to rule of law (*hokumat-e qanuni*), saying that no one was above the laws of the state.[107] This was as much a criticism of the extra-legal position claimed by the *Rahbar*, as of the various institutions of the Islamic Republic dominated by the conservatives that claimed their legitimacy not from the people but either from the revolution or the

Rahbar. Thus, the conservative establishment decided to fight Khatami back, using the constitutional institutions at their disposal. In this, they had the blessings of Khamenei, presumably annoyed at the assault on his office.

The conservatives drew first blood by charging the Mayor of Tehran, Gholam-Hussein Karbaschi with embezzlement of billions and wasting public money on 'dubious development projects'. Karbaschi, who was instrumental to Khatami's campaign in Tehran, was arrested in April 1998 at the instructions of the conservative dominated *Shari'ah* court, which eventually slapped a huge fine on him, sentenced him to five years in prison and debarred him from public office for 10 years.[108] Karbaschi was then replaced by the hard-line populist from the *Basij*, Mahmoud Ahmedinejad, presumably as a price for *basiji* collaboration with the conservative establishment.

This was followed by the impeachment of the reformist Minster of the Interior, Abdullah Nouri. The minister had shown his position clearly by purging his ministry of conservative functionaries, by his refusing to dismiss Karbaschi before he was tried, and finally by publicly endorsing Ayatollah Montazeri's attacks on Khamenei. In June 1998, Nuri was accused of 'inability to maintain social peace' during the Montazeri incident, refusing to arrest Karbaschi and making unsuitable appointments to the ministry: he was impeached by 137 votes in the 270-member *Majlis*, removed from office, and replaced by the moderate MRM leader Abdolwahid Musavi Lari.[109]

The conservative backlash was not limited to resort to legality. The *Mo'talefeh* mobilised a number of extremist right-wing circles with elements from the *Sepah*, the ministry of information, the Islamic judiciary, and the national radio and TV under the alleged leadership of 'Ali Larijani.[110] Ayatollah Muhammad Yazdi, the head of the Islamic judiciary, furnished the right-wing with the religious justification: noting that the new cultural regime with its 'unfettered press' was diluting the *vilayat-e faqih*, he declared that Islam called upon the faithful to stand firm against such subversion of the faith.[111] The *Basijis* were sought to be used by *Mo'talefeh* as the 'physical arm' of the conservatives in intimidating, threatening and even eliminating the reformists. The *Basij* also became highly active in upholding 'moral virtues', attacking university students and less-than-austere youth on the streets, generating a lot of disquiet on the university campuses of Iran. Violent clashes became a regular feature as the reformist students' movement led by the *Tahkim-e Vahdat* decided to stand its ground, by taking on the right-wing vigilantes. Reformist newspapers alleged that the conservatives wanted to create an atmosphere such a degree of disquiet that would require military intervention by the *Sepah*. The allegation seemed on the point of coming true in November 1997 when the deputy of the *Sepah*, Muhammad Baqer Zolqadr, warned that the *Sepah* would not allow the regime be endangered in any way.[112]

Stung by the subtle and unsubtle attacks on his office, 'Ali Khamenei threw in his own weight as the *Rahbar* behind the conservatives. Khamenei took particular exception to the air of cultural freedom that allowed criticism of even the cardinal features of the regime. With his blessing, the Islamic judiciary under Ayatollah Yazdi went on the rampage against reformist publications, shutting these down almost as fast as the Ministry of Culture and Islamic Guidance could issue them licence. Prominent reformist publications *Jame'h* and *Tus* were closed down in September 1998; several national, provincial and local newspapers were shut down between 1998 and 1999. Journalists interrogating a little too deeply into the organisations that constituted conservative strongholds frequently paid a heavy price for their boldness – exemplified by the physical assault on the staff of the *Khordad* in January 1999. Perhaps the deadliest attack on the freedom of speech came in February 1999, when Mohsen Kadivar, a prominent left-wing intellectual and a critic of the absolute character of the *vilayat-e faqih* was sentenced to prison for a year and a half on charges of 'unsettling the public'.[113]

Khatami responded to these attacks on the reform movement in two ways – first, in a public relations victory, in January 1999 he exposed a conservative plot to destabilise the country before mounting its 'stabilisation coup' that entailed the collusion of some high officials in the conservative-dominated intelligence ministry in the murder and physical assault on prominent reformists and intellectuals,[114] and second, and more important, he kept on pressing ahead with whatever reforms he could deliver. Confronted with a *Majlis* that was dominated by the conservatives, even if only marginally, Khatami realised that the more contentious reforms of the establishment could not even be attempted, far less achieved. He thus went for those reforms that would be difficult even for the conservatives to thwart. In February 1999, Khatami delivered on his campaign promise to hold the first ever elections for local governments in Iran: 'at one stroke 2,00,000 democratically elected officials entered the political structure, despite conservative ... efforts to hold back the candidacy of the *Do-e Khordad* candidates'.[115] The successful empowerment of the people put wind in the reformist sail, securing not only a majority of the newly-elected local governments but also a decisive majority in the sixth *Majlis* elections of 2000.

Despite the usual debarring of left-wing and centrist candidates by the Guardians, in the sixth *Majlis*, the reformist *Dovvom-e Khordad* coalition secured 65 per cent of the votes, and 189 of the 270 *Majlis* seats; the conservatives got 19 per cent of the votes and 54 seats with 42 going to the independents. The reformist victory more or less completed the elected-unelected divide in Iranian body-politic with the balance of power in all elective institutions being held by the reformists and all non-elective organisations being dominated by the conservatives. In 2001, Khatami himself secured a victory even more resounding than the first one. Unlike Rafsanjani, who won his second term with a reduced vote share, Khatami actually increased his tally of votes to 78.3 per cent of the total. For all practical purposes, this constituted the high point of the reform movement under Khatami, because ever since the sixth *Majlis* came into being the conservative establishment dug its heels in opposition to Khatami every step of the way.

The determined character of conservative opposition had as much to do with the economic reforms that Khatami was advocating as with his proposed political reforms. Khatami had two years at his disposal to come up with any original economic plan, with the Second Five Year Plan still running as he came to power. In August 1998, a year ahead of the Third Plan, Khatami was forced to introduce an 'Economic Recovery Plan', which paid special attention to the issue of unemployment. While on the one hand the document emphasised the need for civil society reforms for stable economic growth (viz. observance of existing economic regulations, attention to transparency in business practices), it had also tried to let the genie out of the bottle by undertaking the task of 'breaking monopolies' and regulating the *bonyads*.[116] The challenge was resumed in course of the Third Five Year Plan, introduced in the second half of 1999 and passed by the *Majlis* as well as the Guardians in 2000. While most of the package was essentially a continuation of the economic liberalisation programme of the Rafsanjani era (viz. macroeconomic regulation, encouragement of domestic and foreign investment, reduction of public sector in the economy), the Third Plan renewed the emphasis on making the giant economic entities of the *Bonyad* fully accountable and open to public scrutiny.[117] Khatami's attack on the *bonyads* won the most (probably the only) significant victory in July 1999, when Mohsen Rafiqdust, the influential director of the wealthiest *bonyad*, the *Bonyad-e Mostazafin*, had to be replaced after being continuously shielded by Khamenei throughout the Rafsanjani era. His replacement, former minister of defence Muhammad Foruzandeh, had to pledge cooperation with the government.[118] As international oil prices, (hence, oil revenue, the mainstay of the Iranian government) continued to fall consistently during the Khatami years, the reformists ceaselessly attacked the virtual drain of government subsidies into similar other *bonyads* as well (viz. *Astan-e Qods* foundation) and demanded accountability of such organisations to the elected functionaries of the people.[119] As almost all of these *bonyads* are connected personally or organisationally with either the *Rahbar*, and/or the conservative establishment, particularly the *Sepah*, the reformist agenda understandably alarmed the conservatives as an attempt to undermine their material basis. The Guardians, accordingly, threw out a *Majlis* bill in 2001 that proposed to enable the *Majlis* to appoint a committee of audit on the activities of the *Bonyad-e Mostazafin*, saying it infringed the autonomy granted to the foundation by the *Rahbar* himself.

By the autumn of 2002, it was fairly clear that the *Dovvom-e Khordad* movement had been successfully stonewalled in its quest for structural reforms; both physical violence and use of institutional leverage by the conservatives undermined the willingness and ability of the reformists to carry the struggle forward. Despite the fact that Khatami's sincerity to the reformist cause was never quite questioned, the effectiveness of his strategy of changing the system from within came under major criticism from all sides. Khatami's failure to push reform was blamed squarely on the polycratic structure of Iranian body-politic with its potential institutional gridlock, which therefore took the wind out of the reformist sail.

Since its inauguration in 2000, the sixth *Majlis* attempted to introduce a broad range of legislation – ranging from women's rights to human rights, from press freedom to increasing the potency of *Majlis* as the supreme legislative body in Iran. The reformists tried to revise laws about representation of the people, regarding parliamentary immunity for *Majlis* deputies vis-a-vis *Shari'ah* courts, according equal property rights to men and women, etc. More than fifty of such major attempts at reforming the Islamic Republic have been successfully blocked by the Guardians.[120] Since no bill becomes a law without the consent of the Guardians, reformist domination of the *Majlis* by itself did not signify any paramountcy over the legislative process. Towards the end of 2003, stonewalled by the Guardians at every step, Khatami introduced two bills of some significance. One of these bills proposed to authorise the President to identify violations of the constitution and take the responsible people/institutions to higher courts of law. This bill, in effect, vested in the President powers equal to the Guardians to pronounce on the constitutionality of any move. The other bill proposed to remove the power of eliminating 'unsuitable' candidates that had been appropriated by the Guardians. The problem was for both these bills to become law, the Guardians had to approve these, and understandably they chose to reject such curtailment of their own powers.[121]

Indeed, if the Guardians reject a bill, they have to indicate specific objections with respect to Islamic law. If the *Majlis* chooses to revise and amend the bill somewhat and send it back, the Guardians can either ignore the amended bill or reject it outright. This procedure is theoretically meant to take three months at most; in fact occasionally this procedure has been known to have taken more than two years.[122] After having blocked the *Majlis* on every conceivable issue, the Guardians then went on to disqualify more than half of the total applicants for the *Majlis* elections in 2004, excluding almost all prominent reformists. At the end of the process, the conservatives won 156 out of the 290 seats. Significantly, however, the conservative *Mo'talefeh*-JRM axis was joined by a relatively new entrant, the Basij-dominated Islamic populist *E'telaf-e Abadgaran-e Iran-e Islami* (Alliance of Builders of Islamic Iran, usually referred to as the *Abadgaran*) led by the allies of the Mayor of Tehran, Mahmoud Ahmedinejad.

The argument about institutional deadlock has an additional resonance with respect to the role played by the Expediency Council. Chaired by Rafsanjani ever since its creation in 1987, the Expediency Council proved pivotal to resolution of deadlocks between the *Majlis* and the Guardians. Till as late as the end of the term of fifth *Majlis* in 2000, the Expediency Council had occasionally permitted the passage of laws that the Guardians had rejected as contradictory to Islam. During the tenure of the sixth *Majlis*, however, the Expediency Council has invariably sided with the Guardians against the reformist camp.[123]

While such a pro-conservative stand of the Expediency Council has been explained by analysts in terms of its predominantly conservative composition, such analysis fails to account for the incremental opposition of Rafsanjani to Khatami's reform agenda.[124] A more pertinent explanation could be the split within the reformist platform in the *Majlis* during Khatami's second term, which Rafsanjani presumably sought to capitalise on in order to further his personal prospects for a third presidential term.

The reformist coalition in the sixth *Majlis* was dominated no longer by the left-wing elements of the MRM, rather by the decidedly centrist *Jebhe-ye Sherikat-e Iran-e Islami* (Islamic Iran Participation Front) and the *Kargozaran*. However, the leftwing elements represented by the MRM, the *Mojahedin-e Inqilab-e Islami* and the *Hizb-e Zahmatkashan-e Iran* remained sufficiently influential to prevent any rapid liberalisation of the economy. This made Khatami's second term in office quite difficult because of the veritable economic crisis that Iran was facing at the moment. With the global decline in the price of oil, Iran was earning an average price of US$ 9.50, as against the average of US$ 12 per barrel projected for the duration of the third plan. As against an average oil income of US$ 9-12 billion, the projected import bill was set at US$ 14 billion, with provision for its upward revision subsequently.[125] In this context of economic hardship, Khatami decided to step up the structural adjustment policies recommended by World Bank and IMF during the Rafsanjani era, and launched a charm offensive aimed at accomplishing normalisation of relations with the west, especially the US that had been begun by Rafsanjani. Khatami's 'constructive engagement' with the EU was rapidly followed with feelers being sent out by his foreign minister, Kamal Kharrazi to the US, so that normal relations with Washington DC could be restored. In return it was hoped that the US opposition to Iran's entry in the WTO would be dropped, Iran would become integrated into the world economy and that the resultant expansion of the country's economic horizons would help the embattled economy recover. Tehran's gestures of solidarity with the US after the 9/11 tragedy increased the hopes of such normalisation.[126]

The positive response Khatami received from Europe, known as 'constructive engagement', strengthened his hand in the arena of Iran's domestic politics to such an extent that he and his foreign minister Kamal Kharrazi were able to push vigorously for a revision of many of the cardinal postulates of Tehran's foreign policy, including the confrontationalist posture that Tehran had maintained towards the US Fresh grounds, very clearly, were being broken when Khatami spoke of the imperative of *Guftogu-ye Tamaddunha* (Dialogue of Civilisations) during his address to the UN General Assembly in September 1998.[127] Candlelight vigils taken out in Tehran after the tragic events of 9/11 indicated the strength of the positive vibes Khatami had unleashed, increasing the hopes of such normalisation. When US invaded Afghanistan to topple the Taliban regime, Tehran cooperated extensively with Washington and was instrumental in promoting the Karzai-Northern Alliance coalition. In January 2002, Tehran pledged US$ 540 million (as against US$ 290 million pledged by US) at an international donors' conference; Tehran even volunteered to train 20,000 Afghan soldiers under the US leadership.[128]

Khatami sought to use the overtures in January 2002 as an opening gambit in normalisation of relations with Washington, but opponents of Khatami tried to undermine such overtures with arms shipments to Palestine. Two weeks later, President Bush's 'Axis of Evil' speech made no mention of Iranian contribution in Afghanistan. This was seen in Tehran widely as an indication that Khatami's olive branch was being spurned. Nevertheless, as the US began to move against Iraq, Khatami and Kharrazi pressed for cooperation with the US. At one stage, Khatami and Kharrazi even considered allowing US the use of Iranian airspace for operations against Iraq, because by weakening Iraq, the US was in a way serving Tehran's interests.[129]

But the dynamics of domestic politics prompted the Rahbar (Supreme Leader) 'Ali Khamenei to go against such cooperation, citing the Axis of Evil Speech as his evidence of American feelings towards Iran, foiling Khatami-Kharrazi duo. The US' discovery of evidence indicating Tehran's nuclear weapons programme and the consequent international pressure on Tehran, coming as it did alongside the ouster of Saddam, gave Khatami his last opportunity to bring about reconciliation. He suspended the nuclear programme pending resolution of the issue by negotiation with the IAEA, hoping that Tehran's nuclear weapons programme being in its infancy such resolution would not be difficult.[130] Once that happens, normalisation of relations with the international community could follow with some ease. However, by 2004, there was a growing consensus in Tehran that the US was not responding to any of Iran's conciliatory gestures. Presidential hopeful, 'Ali Larijani, attacked the concessions made by Rowhani under instructions from the President, compelling Khatami to resume some of the suspended nuclear activity, but stopping well short of uranium enrichment, which remained an extended olive branch even after Tehran began to harden diplomatic positions with the EU-3 in 2004.[131] The writing on the wall, however, was clear: Khatami had lost the gambit, opening the way for the brinkmanship that characterised the negotiations during the era of Ahmedinejad.

In the domestic arena, Khatami's escalation of the pace of liberalisation caused rifts within the *Dowom-e Khordad* front itself. Accordingly, by 2002-03 Khatami had to begin placating the left-wing statist elements in his coalition, renewing his commitment to some expensive social security and welfare packages, which could not be paid without adding to the steep inflationary pressure on the economy.[132] By 2003, therefore, the *Kargozaran* support for Khatami began to diminish; animosity towards reformism began to grow in the *bazaar* as well. Most significantly, Khatami's populist support base diminished significantly: the populist constituency in general and the urban and rural poor in particular deserted the reformists by voting with the *Basij*-dominated socially conservative but populist outfit, the *Abadgaran* in the 2003 local government elections. Khatami might conceivably still have pulled it off if he succeeded in the direction of political reforms, which would have included clipping the wings of the Expediency Council also. However, Rafsanjani, the original architect of the political centre in Iranian politics, was resolved to push forward with the economic liberalisation, if he could secure a third term as President when Khatami stepped down in 2005. It was essential for him that Khatami's success should be tempered somewhat, so that he would be left with an agenda to pursue.[133] Hence, in course of Khatami's second term, the Expediency Council under Rafsanjani openly aligned with the Guardians not to expedite legislation but to impede it. Accordingly, the centrist political combination that had been forged gradually through the decade of the 1990s was split open.

In the presidential election of 2005, the factional nature of Iranian politics appeared in full force. The centrist political platform, which had emerged during the second term of Rafsanjani and flourished under Khatami, split up to field at least three prominent candidates: Akbar Hashmi Rafsanjani was fielded by the centre-right *Kargozaran*, Mostafa Moeen by the centrist Islamic Iran Participation Front and Mehdi Karroubi by the centre-left MRM. The conservatives too split between the *Mo'talefeh*-JRM axis (backed by Khamenei himself) and the *Basij*-dominated populist outfit, the *Abadgaran*. The *Mo'talefeh*-JRM axis nominated the former minister of Culture and Islamic Guidance, 'Ali Larijani, for presidency, while the *Abadgaran* nominated the Mayor of Tehran, Mahmoud Ahmedinejad. In the first round, Rafsanjani emerged in the lead (21.13 per cent votes), followed closely by Ahmedinejad (19.43 per cent); in the run-off second round, Ahmedinejad (61.69 per cent) trounced Rafsanjani (35.93 per cent) by a margin of over 7 million votes. Rafsanjani accused the conservative establishment of rigging the polls in favour of Ahmedinejad, but despite several reported electoral irregularities, the reason for the outcome lies elsewhere. Dismayed by the stonewalling that greeted the reformists and Khatami's failure to handle that, a large number of Iranians simply stayed away from the polls. In the 2005 election, only 29.5 million Iranians turned out to vote in the first round, that is, 62.66 per cent of the eligible voters; in the second round, the turn-out fell still further to about 27.9 million (59.6 per cent). While Ahmedinejad presumably managed to consolidate the social conservative *and* the populist components of the Iranian electorate,

Rafsanjani failed to consolidate the reformist vote having lost his credibility to the centrist and left-of-centre voters.[134]

VI. Conclusion

The centrist political platform that emerged during the Rafsanjani years and then flourished under Khatami was the result of a conscious break with the extreme positions on economy and society that characterised the post-revolutionary regime. Once the exigencies of the Iraq war disappeared, the rigidly statist postures of regulated economy and a highly restrictive social order had to be dismantled. At this juncture, the twin processes of economic and socio-political liberalisation that characterised the reformist movement generated two apparently contradictory impulses: in economics, the Iranian reformists wanted to move *away from* the general leftist preference for an economy regulated by the state; by contrast in socio-political sphere, the reformists sought to move *towards* the general leftist position of individual freedom. The failure of the Khatami era to prove the mixed economic model as the panacea for Iran's economic woes has temporarily split the reformist camp into the centre-right and the centre-left. Further, Khatami's failure to bring about any major structural reform in the Islamic Republic has depleted the ranks of those who have no patience with a restrictive socio-political order. The centrist political platform, thus, came into being in response to a set of problems, and has received a setback because it has failed to tackle those problems affectively.

The failure of the reformist movement has frequently been attributed, with some justification, to the polycratic institutional character of the Islamic regime. However, to argue that the system is incapable of transmutation is to ignore the fact that the polycratic nature of the system itself in its present form is the result of political evolution of the Islamic Republic. Khatami's approach to structural reform clearly indicated an awareness of the possibilities of such mutation not only within the broad constitutional parameters set down in 1979, but also beyond these. His failure is suggestive not of the impossibility of reform, rather of the specific manner in which it was sought to be implemented in the backdrop of factional politics and an embattled economy.

It is probably too early to attempt an analysis of the Ahmedinejad era. What can be said with some certainty is that, contrary to the popular perception, despite his social conservatism, President Ahmedinejad is in no more harmony with the conservative establishment led by the *Rahbar* 'Ali Khamenei than his reformist predecessor – a fact borne out by his increasing isolation within the Iranian establishment after the disputed presidential elections of 2009. Nor is the populist economic approach of the President proving anywhere nearly as promising as the liberalisation of the Rafsanjani-Khatami years. The oil revenue windfall provided by the surge in global crude prices from 2006 onwards has merely staved off an impending economic disaster, but Ahmedinejad has been severely criticised for his disastrous populism at home and abroad. As the effect of the incremental economic sanctions of 2010 and then 2011 by the US and the EU begin to tell upon the Iranian economy in the background of the global economic slowdown since 2008, the populism that had sustained Ahmedinejad during his first term has become unsustainable in the long run. Ahmedinejad paid the price with virtual decimation of his associates in the *Majlis* elections of 2011. The economic condition of Iran today being considerably more dire than what it was during the Khatami era, the fact of the control of the Iranian economy by the *bonyad-ha* is resented more than when Khatami wanted to have these audited. The *bazaar*, considerably weaker but nevertheless a formidable economic force, has continued to suffer from the relentless rise of the Sepah during the Ahmedinejad era. It is, thus, probably not an exaggeration to say that Ahmedinejad's second term has come to underline the need for a change in the long-term direction of Iranian economy, and this need is being increasingly appreciated across the political spectrum.

There is also a growing awareness within the conservative establishment that the Islamic regime can not persist in marginalising the vibrant and youthful population of the country in the name of a revolution that an overwhelming majority had either not seen or cannot remember. The so-called Arab Spring has only reinforced this awareness, and the crackdown which followed the disputes over Ahmedinejad's re-election seem to have been more like the leftovers from a bygone era, than an indicator of things to come. If the two extremist political platforms do not themselves move to the centre in the medium term, the resurgence of the political centre in Iran appears to be only a matter of time.

Notes and References

a   I would like to acknowledge a number of professional and amateur observers of Iranian politics who have contributed to my own understanding of post-revolutionary Iranian politics. They are Reza Alijani, Asef Bayat, Kaveh Bayat, Muhammad Fayyaz-Bakhsh, Sayyid Akhtar Hussain, Habib Khalilee, John Limbert, Muhammad Malijoo, Misagh Parsa, Fatemeh Sadeghi, Morhad Sagefi, Nahid Tavassoli and Methraveh Tavassoli. I would also like to put on record my appreciation for the Maulana Abul Kalam Azad Institute of Asian Studies, who funded my field trip to Iran in 2006, and the Centre for Pakistan and West Asian Studies, Calcutta University, but for whose support this work would not have been possible.

1. See, for instance, Mehdi Moslem, *Factional Politics in Post-Khomeini Iran*. (New York: Syracuse University Press, 2002); Hossein S. Seifzadeh, 'The Landscape of Factional Politics and its Future in Iran', *Middle East Journal*, vol. 57, no. 1, Winter 2003, pp. 57-75; Roy Tekeyh, 'Iran at a Crossroads', vol. 57, no. 1, Winter 2003, pp. 42-56; Mehrangiz Kar, 'Constitutional Constraints', *Journal of Democracy*, vol. 14, no. 1, 'Deadlock in Iran', January 2003, pp. 132-36.

2. Behzad Yaghmayian, *Social Change in Iran: An Eye-witness Account of Dissent, Dissidence and New Movement for Rights*, (New York, SUNY, 2002); Ramin Jahanbegloo, 'Pressures from Below', *Journal of Democracy*, vol. 14, no. 1, 'Deadlock in Iran', January 2003, pp. 126-31.

3. According to the Constitution of 1906, the monarchy in Iran was reduced to only executive authority; it was divested of its legislative functions that were made over to the popularly elected *Majlis* (Parliament); an independent judiciary was also ordained. The principles of separation of powers, popular sovereignty and rule of law instituted by the 1906 constitution were intended to safeguard interests of the people by making abuse of executive authority difficult.

4. For a critical account of the Pahlavi era in Iran, see Ervand Abrahamian, *Iran between Two Revolutions*, (Princeton, NJ: Princeton University Press, 1982), Homa Katouzian, *The Political Economy of Modern Iran: Despotism and Pseudo-Modernism 1926-79*, (London and New York: Macmillan and New York University Press, 1981).

5. The first *Rahbar*, Ayatollah Khomeini, was raised to the office by virtue of the leadership role he played during the struggle against the Shah. Subsequent holders of the office have to be elected by the Assembly of Experts in accordance with the qualifications laid down in Article 109 of the constitution. As the Experts in their turn have to be directly elected by the people, it is theoretically possible to argue that the *Rahbar* is indirectly representative of the people.

6. See, Articles 107-112 of the constitution of the Islamic Republic of Iran.

7. The powers of the President are laid down in Articles 113-32 of the Constitution of the Islamic Republic.
8. During 1979-89, the President was the titular head of the executive wing of the government. The de facto head of the executive was the Prime Minister – answerable to the *Majlis* for the conduct of the whole council of ministers which he headed. During the Presidency of 'Ali Khamenei, the office of the Prime Minister was held by Hussein-Musavi. In 1989, upon Khamenei becoming the *Rahbar* and Rafsanjani's rise to the Presidency, the post of the Prime Minister was abolished.
9. In order to ensure participation of non-Muslim religious minorities, article 64 of the Constitution provides for the Jews and Zoroastrians to elect a representative each, one for the Assyrian and Chaldean Christians together and two for the Armenians.
10. Similar elective executive functionaries and legislative councils exist at the provincial and municipal levels as well, although their powers and responsibilities are very carefully circumscribed, and the election process is seldom as direct as it is in the election of the President. The Mayor of Tehran, for instance, governing a city that contains nearly a fifth of the total population of the country, is one of the most powerful executive offices of the country. But his authority is very carefully circumscribed to issues largely of only local administrative character.
11. Six of its members are just *fuqaha* (Islamic jurists) 'conscious of present needs', who are appointed to the body by the *Rahbar*; the other six are lay jurists specialising in different branches of law, selected by the Majlis from a list of Muslim jurists nominated by the Head of the judiciary. The members are elected for terms of six years, with a third retiring each year.
12. According to Article 96 of the Constitution, the Islamic character of any measure is pronounced upon by majority vote of the *fuqaha* in the Council. The constitutionality of any measure is pronounced upon by a majority vote of all members of the Council.
13. Asghar Schirazi, *The Constitution of Iran: Politics and State in the Islamic Republic*, [translated by John O'Hara], (London: I.B. Tauris, 1997), p. 64.
14. For a comprehensive treatment on this issue, see Misagh Parsa, *the Social Origins of the Islamic Revolution* (New Brunswick and London: Rutgers University Press, 1989).
15. For a description of the major industrial families under the Shah and the process of nationalisation, see Anourshivan Ehteshami, *After Khomeini: the Iranian Second Republic*, (London: Routledge, 1995), pp. 83-88.
16. Suzanne Maloney, 'Agents or Obstacles: Parastatal Foundations and Challenges for Iranian Development', in Parvin Alizadeh, *The Economy of Iran: Dilemmas of an Islamic State*, (London and New York: I. B. Tauris, 2000), p. 154.
17. For an account of the impact of the war on Iran See David Menasheri, *Iran: a Decade of War and Revolution*, (New York: Holmes and Meier, 1990).
18. Bank Markazi, *Hesabha-ye Melli-ye Iran, 1353-66*, (Tehran: Bank Markazi, 1991), cited in Sohrab Behdad, 'From Populism to Liberalism: the Iranian Predicament', in

Alizadeh, *the Economy of Iran*, pp. 103, 109.
19. See, Michael Eisenstadt, "The Armed Forces of the Islamic Republic of Iran: An Assessment, "*Middle East Review of International Affairs Journal*, vol. 5, no. 1, March 2001.
20. *Bonyads* are a variation of a *wqaf* (sing. *waqf.*) i.e, autonomous charitable foundations in Muslim societies relying upon endowments by faithful, purported to provide material support to the less-privileged members of the Muslim community. Associated generally with religious shrines and orders, organisations such as the *Bonyad-e Astan-e Qods* or the *Bonyad-e Panzdah-ye Khordad* have prospered under the Islamic Republic. For instance, based at the shrine of Imam Reza in Mashhad, owning property all over Iran and receiving a steady stream of revenue from alms paid by pilgrims, the *Bonyad-e Astan-e Qods* is supposed to have an annual budget of around US$ 2 billion. The Islamic Republic, however, has invested far greater assets to *bonyads* that have no attachment with religious endowments. While there are some foundations that rely on private funds, most rely heavily on the government for either direct subsidies or special prerogatives, with considerable autonomy. Several of such quasi-public foundations, such as *Bonyad-e Mostazafin wa Janbaz* (Foundation for the Oppressed and the Self-Sacrificers, entrusted with protecting victims of the revolution and the war), the *Komiteh-ye Imdad-e Imam* (Imam's Relief Committee, providing medical, educational and social assistance to needy rural families), *Jihad-e Sazandegi* (Reconstruction Crusade, responsible for promotion of economic development in the countryside) were pivotal to sustained war effort and also economic activity all through the 1980s
21. The *Mostazafin* was set up in March 1979, through a decree issued by Khomeini himself. The organisation immediately absorbed the Pahlavi Foundation, with assets of nearly US$ 3.2 billion; later it absorbed some of the assets of 51 of the largest industrialists when the regime began nationalisation of émigré properties. See, For a case study of the *Mostazafin*, see Maloney, 'Agents or Obstacles', pp. 153-66; See also, Farhad Kazemi, 'Civil Society and Iranian Politics' in A.R. Norton, *Civil Society in the Middle East*, vol. 2, (New York: E.J. Brill, 1996), pp. 141-146.
22. *Resalat,* June 18, 1987.
23. Perhaps the most ironic of the lot was the issue of August 1981 bill on land reform. The bill, which proposed to distribute land among landless peasants, kicked up quite a controversy because Khomeini himself had opposed as un-Islamic a similar reform proposed by Shah in 1963. The Guardians rejected the bill citing the Qur'anic injunction that Muslims should have mandate over their possessions, almost echoing Khomeini's position in 1963. Rafsanjani, who favoured the legislation, sought Khomeini's intercession on this matter admitting that it might be opposed to a literal reading of the Islamic laws. Khomeini then approved the bill, saying such an act is permissible because the survival of the Islamic regime might depend on it. See, Mehdi Moslem, *Factional Politics in Post-Khomeini Iran*, p. 64. For a detailed treatment of the question, see Khadija V. Frings-Hessami, 'The Islamic Debate about Land Reform in the Iranian Parliament, 1981-86', in *Middle Eastern*

Studies, vol. 37, no. 4, October 2001, pp. 136-181.
24. Moslem, *Factional Politics*, pp. 49-50.
25. Cited in Ibid., p. 64.
26. Ibid., pp. 72-73.
27. Ibid., pp. 67-68.
28. *Ittela'at*, January 9, 1988.
29. *Resalat*, January 12, 1988.
30. *Ittela'at*, December 31, 1987.
31. *Ittela'at*, October 5, 1988.
32. *Ittela'at*, February 20, 1989.
33. The Assembly for Reappraisal of the Constitution was appointed by Khomeini with complete disregard for the elective principle. Only 10 of its 66 members were elected in the sense they were deputies of the *majlis*; other members included those of the Guardians, the Expediency Council, representatives of the judiciary, etc. See Asghar Schirazi, *the Constitution of Iran*, pp. 64-65.
34. Ibid., pp. 104-05.
35. Sohrab Behdad, 'From Populism to Liberalism', p. 113.
36. *Kayhan Havaii*, August 24, 1991.
37. For a study of the First Five-Year Plan, see M.R. Ghasimi, 'Iranian Economy after the Revolution: an Economic Appraisal of the Five year Plan, *International Journal of the Middle East Studies*, 24/4, 1992.
38. Sohrab Behdad, 'From Populism to Liberalism', p. 114.
39. Bijan Khajehpour, 'Iran's Economy: Twenty Years after the Islamic Revolution', p. 97.
40. For a very comprehensive treatment of Iran's economic liberalisation under Rafsanjani, see Sohrab Behdad, 'From Populism to Liberalism', pp. 115-31.
41. Moslem, *Factional Politics*, pp. 163-164.
42. *Bayan*, June-July 1990, p. 39.
43. Moslem, *Factional Politics*, p. 165.
44. The *Sepah* remains as a self-contained set of units comprising ground, naval and air forces around 1,25,000 strong within the *Artesh*, but commanded by its own Chief Commander. Apart from the 1,25,000 regular *Pasdaran*, it is supposed to control the 90,000 regular and 3,00,000 reservists of the *Bassij*.
45. Moslem, *Factional Politics*, p. 191.
46. Ibid., p. 171.
47. *Salaam*, November 24, 1992.
48. 'Culture, Islamic Guidance Minister on Policies', broadcast May 03, 1992, FBIS-NES-92-105, June 01, 1992.
49. *Salam*, March 17, 1991.
50. Previously, to be elected to the Experts, eligible candidates needed to be fully acquainted with the basis of *ijtihad* (independent legal reasoning) and educated at prominent *howzeh* (seminaries) 'to the degree of being able to discern competency for the *marja'iyat* and *Rahbariyat*.' The eligibility of candidates was discerned by

attestation of three well-known teachers of *howzeh*, or by general recognition of the candidates as a *mujtahid* (capable of independent legal reasoning) in religious circles, or attestation from the *Rahbar* himself. After the changes brought in 1990, it was sufficient for the candidates to be eligible to infer on issues of *fiqh* (Islamic jurisprudence), which would be subject to a competency test evaluated by the Guardians. Secondly, attestation by prominent teachers of the *howzeh* was no longer acceptable; either the leader or the *fuqaha* among the Guardians had to testify to a candidate's eligibility. See, Moslem, *Factional Politics*, pp. 156-157.

51. Ibid., p. 159.
52. *Salaam,* March 10, 1992.
53. *Salaam,* February 24, 1992.
54. Moslem, *Factional Politics*, p. 184.
55. Khatami went on to head the *Kitabkhaneh-ye Melli* (National Library) and functioned as an advisor to Rafsanjani on his cultural policy. Moslem, *Factional Politics*. p. 175.
56. *Ittela'at,* December 31, 1992.
57. *Kayhan,* April 12, 1993.
58. *Kayhan,* September 30, 1993.
59. Moslem, *Factional Politics*, p. 217.
60. All the data in this section are derived from M. Hakim Pesaran, 'Economic Trends and Macro-Economic Policies in Post-Revolutionary Iran', in Alizadeh, *The Economy of Iran*, p. 67.
61. Ibid., p. 72.
62. Ibid., p. 69.
63. Moslem, *Factional Politics,* pp. 187-89
64. Utility charges for telephone, post, water and electricity were increased dramatically. Postal costs increased by 100 per cent. A flat 5 per cent custom duty was imposed on all imported merchandise.
65. Moslem, *Factional Politics,* p. 198.
66. *Ittela'at,* June 13, 1993.
67. Moslem, *Factional Politics,* p. 204.
68. Ibid., p. 206.
69. *Ittela'at*, February 02, 1994.
70. *Resalat*, November 23, 1994.
71. Moslem, *Factional Politics*, pp. 209-210.
72. *Salaam,* December 5, 1994. The government-run *Refah* (Welfare) chain-stores were founded principally by the three banks *Melli, Tejarat* and *Saderat* along with the municipal government of Tehran and the state run insurance companies *Alborz* and *Asia*. The *Refah* stores engaged in direct competition with the retail trade of the *bazaar*. The initiative also implied redirecting the flow of capital away from the *bazaar* into public sector banks, thus impacting on the financial health and autonomy of the *bazaar*.
73. Farhang Rajaee, in conversation with the author, April 2004.
74. In the social life of modern Iranians, 'heading out for the open' constitutes a fairly

regular part. At the weekends as much as during holidays, Iranians tend to head for open public spaces, to let the hair down, as it were. The municipal parks became tremendously popular for these purposes from the 1990s. The parks were also popular among people who want to meet without the fear of being snooped upon. Couples engaged in courtship, young people engaging in flirtation, friends relaxing with boardgames, musicians playing instruments, families relaxing with children – all these became regular sights at the municipal parks.

75. *Salaam*, June 24, 1993.
76. *Salaam*, July 03, 1993.
77. Moslem, *Factional Politics*, p. 219.
78. See, for instance, *Ittela'at*, October 29, 1992.
79. *Ittela'at*, November 05, 1992.
80. Ittela'at, October 05, 1993.
81. Moslem, *Factional Politics*, p. 221.
82. Ibid.
83. Ibid., pp. 221-223.
84. See for instance, *Asr-e Ma*, December 03, 1995.
85. *Jahan-e Islam*, June 11, 1994.
86. The fifteen included stalwarts like Rafsanjani's legal adviser Ayatollah Mohajerani, former minister of economics and head of Bank Markazi , Mohsen Nurbakhsh; Minister of economics Morteza Muhammad Khan; head of Atomic energy, Reza Amrollahi and the Mayor of Tehran, Gholam-Hossein Karbaschi.
87. *Hamshahri*, January 20, 1996.
88. *Hamshahri*, March 24, 1996.
89. *Resalat*, February 19, 1996.
90. Moslem, *Factional Politics*, pp. 238-240.
91. Geneive Abdo and Jonathan Lyons, *Answering only to God: Faith and Freedom in Twentieth Century Iran*, (New York: Henry Holt and Co, 2003), p. 62.
92. *Salaam*, October 27, 1996.
93. Abdo and Lyons, *Answering only to God*, pp. 57-58.
94. See for instance, *Jahan-e Islam*, November 06, 1996.
95. *Hamshahri*, April 13, 1997. After Hussein-Musavi stood down, the *Kargozaran* actually considered running some of its own members for the nomination, but having no real social base beyond some technocrats failed to put anyone up. Rafsanjani himself never fancied Khatami's chances of defeating Nateq-Nouri, but was hopeful that Khatami might be able to drag him to a second-round of polls, which would have weakened the President and increased Rafsanjani's leverage as the chairman of the Expediency Council. Hence he too supported eventual *Kargozaran* decision to back Khatami.
96. Abdo and Lyons, *Answering only to God*, pp. 58-59.
97. *Salaam*, November 28, 1997.
98. Abdo and Lyons, *Answering only to God*, p. 65.
99. Arang Keshavarzian, *Bazaar and State in Iran: the Politics of the Tehran Marketplace*,

(Cambridge: Cambridge University Press, 2007), p. 268.
100. Abdo and Lyons, *Answering only to God*, p. 86. An internal survey of the *Sepah* revealed that 70 per cent of the rank and file of the *Sepah*, and around 80 per cent of the *basij* supported Khatami in the 1997 elections. *Iran News*, November 16, 1997.
101. *Resalat*, May 26, 1997.
102. *Salaam*, May 28, 1997.
103. Moslem, *Factional Politics*, p. 255.
104. Ibid., p. 256.
105. *Salaam*, October 31, 1997.
106. Moslem, *Factional Politics*, p. 257.
107. *Resalat*, August 25, 1997.
108. Moslem, *Factional Politics*, p. 259. Rafsanjani's manoeuvring behind the scenes eventually succeeded in reducing Karbaschi's prison term to two years.
109. Ibid., pp. 260-261.
110. Ibid., p. 261.
111. Ibid., p. 262.
112. Ibid., pp. 261-262.
113. Ibid., pp. 262-263.
114. Kaveh Ehsani, 'Do-e Khordad and the Spectre of Democracy, *Middle East Report*, No. 212, Pushing the Limits: Iran's Islamic Revolution at Twenty. (Autumn, 1999), p.11.
115. Ibid., p. 11.
116. Bijan Khajehpour, 'Iran's Economy: Twenty Years after the Islamic Revolution,' *After Khomeini*, p. 114.
117. For a brief but comprehensive treatment of the Third Plan, see Khajehpour, 'Iran's Economy', pp. 114-119.
118. Suzanne Maloney, 'Agents or Obstacles?' p. 167.
119. In 2001, these *bonyads* operated hundreds of companies, receive more than half of the state's annual expenditures in terms of economic activities, and account for up to 40 per cent of the country's economy. See, Maloney.
120. Ali Rezaei, 'Last Effort of Iran's Reformists', *Middle East Report*, no. 226, Spring, 2003, p. 41.
121. Ibid., p. 45.
122. Mehrangiz Kar, 'Constitutional Constraints', *Journal of Democracy*, volume 14, Number 1, 'Deadlock in Iran', January 2003, p. 134.
123. Ibid., p. 135.
124. See, for instance, Mehrangiz Kar, 'Constitutional Constraints'.
125. Sohrab Behdad, 'From Populism to Liberalism', p. 135.
126. Even when the US was preparing to invade Iraq, Kharrazi ignored repeated the US violations of Iranian airspace in the run-up to the war. This provided Khamenei, Rafsanjani and other opponents of Khatami's reforms to scuttle the gestures of normalisation. www.ips.net/iranwalksonice/html

127. For an account of Iran's engagement with the UN during the Khatami era, see Koroush Ahmadi, "Iran and the United Nations during Khatami's Presidency", *The Iranian Journal of International Relations*, vol. XVIII, no. 1, 2005, pp. 21-51.
128. James Dobbins, "Negotiating with Iran: Reflections from Personal Experience," *The Washington Quarterly*, 33:1, January 2010, pp. 155-156.
129. Even when the US was preparing to invade Iraq, Kharrazi ignored repeated US violations of Iranian airspace in the run-up to the war. This provided Khamenei, Rafsanjani and other opponents of Khatami's reforms to scuttle the gestures of normalisation. www.ips.net/iranwalksonice/html
130. Tehran's nuclear programme (civilian and/or military) has been the one common strand running through the domestic and foreign policies during the Rafsanjani (conservative-pragmatist), Khatami (liberal-reformist) and Ahmedinejad (conservative-hard-line) eras. Initiated under Rafsanjani during the 1990s with full support of the conservative forces that dominated Tehran's defence establishment, pace of the programme was escalated forth clandestinely till its existence was revealed in 2003 during the Khatami era. Under intense international pressure, the Khatami administration suspended the weapons related activities of the nuclear programme, and negotiated with the EU-3 (European foreign ministers), accepting the Additional Protocol and suspended enrichment of uranium voluntarily.
131. Shahram Chubin, "The Iranian Nuclear Riddle after June 12," *The Washington Quarterly*, 33:1, January 2010, pp. 166-167.
132. Ibid., p. 135.
133. This opinion is quite current among the small Islamic socialist faction of the *Melli Mazhabi* that remained true to the Islamic socialist ideas of Musavi years. Even left-leaning intellectuals like Morhad Saghefi and academics like Muhammad Malijoo shared the same opinion in conversation with the author in Tehran, June 2006.
134. Asef Bayat, in conversation with the author in Beirut, December, 2005.

www.ingramcontent.com/pod-product-compliance
Lightning Source LLC
Chambersburg PA
CBHW020628300426
44112CB00010B/1236